Praise for *I'll Never Be French*

"[F]unny, uplifting and delightful memoir of how [Greenside] learns to love the ways of the French people (without necessarily understanding their customs), without a good working knowledge of their language. . . . This book is recommended to anyone who has been to France, or wants to go to France."
—*The Herald-Sun* (Durham–Chapel Hill, NC)

"Greenside tells a charming story about growing wiser, humbler and more human through home owning in a foreign land."

—*Publishers Weekly*

"Charming . . . a tribute to trusting one's fellow humans and to

urnal

"I   ilari-
o   inst
h   Iark
G   t all
m   ner
w   and
hi   d to
fi

nicle

"I   way
hi   lute
dr   an-
sw   led
Fr   ion
of

Post

"[F   nd-
su

Booklist

"[A]n entertaining book. . . . It's humorous as [Greenside] deals with cultural differences but also heartwarming in his encounters and growing fondness for the locals."
—*Contra Costa Times*

"One of the nicest of the trillions of books about France."
—Diane Johnson, author of *L'Affaire*, *Le Mariage*, and
Le Divorce

"This tale of how one man accidentally becomes a thoroughly integrated member of a French village is funny, insightful, and winningly self-deprecatory. (My favorite character may be the nervous insurance agent.) And Mark Greenside's version of rudimentary spoken French is actually a good demonstration of how to communicate in a language you don't know!"
—Lydia Davis, author of *Varieties of Disturbance: Stories* and
translator of *In Search of Lost Time* by Marcel Proust

"A light, lighthearted, occasionally very funny romp through a region of France not well represented in the travel literature. With his fresh eye and self-deprecating wit, Greenside sketches a wry, cautionary tale for all those of us who are tempted by adventures in foreign real estate."
—Michael Sanders, author of *From Here, You Can't See Paris: Seasons of a French Village and Its Restaurant*

"Mark Greenside has written a sweet, evocative book about the pleasures and perplexities of buying and owning a house in a small town in France. It's a funny, enlightening journey. Sit back, relax, and enjoy the trip."
—Richard Goodman, author of *French Dirt: The Story of a Garden in the South of France*

"Buy This Book, especially if you have traveled to Europe and wondered, as you walked through little, picture-postcard-perfect towns, 'What would it be like to buy a little place here?'"
—James Rowen, thepoliticalenvironment.blogspot.com

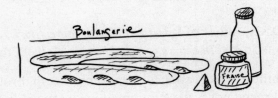

I'll Never Be French
(no matter what I do)

✤ ✤ ✤

*Living in a Small Village
in Brittany*

✤ ✤ ✤

Mark Greenside

Free Press
New York London Toronto Sydney

FREE PRESS

A Division of Simon & Schuster, Inc.
1230 Avenue of the Americas
New York, NY 10020

First Free Press trade paperback edition June 2009

FREE PRESS and colophon are trademarks of
Simon & Schuster, Inc.

For information about special discounts for bulk purchases,
please contact Simon & Schuster Special Sales at
1-866-506-1949 or business@simonandschuster.com

The Simon & Schuster Speakers Bureau can bring authors
to your live event. For more information or to book an event,
contact the Simon & Schuster Speakers Bureau at
1-866-248-3049 or visit our website at www.simonspeakers.com

All illustrations copyright © Kim Thoman
Book design by Ellen R. Sasahara

Manufactured in the United States of America

3   5   7   9   10   8   6   4   2

The Library of Congress has cataloged the hardcover edition as
follows:

Greenside, Mark.
I'll never be French (no matter what I do):
living in a small village in Brittany / Mark Greenside
p. cm.
1. Americans—France—Brittany. 2. Brittany (France)—
Description and travel. 3. Brittany (France)—Social life and
customs. 4. Country life—France—Brittany. I. Title.
DC34.5.A44G74 2008
944'.10839092—dc22
[B]   2008007984

ISBN 978-1-4165-8687-6
ISBN 978-1-4165-8695-1 (pbk)
ISBN 978-1-4165-8713-2 (ebook)

To Kathryn Levy for getting me there,
and Donna Umeki, who makes it better every year;
and to my parents, Dorothy and Ernest Greenside,
for their generosity in everything,
and all my friends in Brittany,
especially Joe and Yvonne B. and their family;
merci, merci, mercy.

A Note to the Reader

It is my fervent wish in writing this book not to create any international incidents or lose any friends. Therefore, the American, English, and Canadian names are actual names (except Sally's), because those people generally like being singled out. Most of the French names, including some of the places, are fictionalized, because those people generally do not.

Contents

Getting There

It begins with a girl. It always begins with a girl, and even though we don't make it through the summer—through even *half* the summer—she gets me there and changes my life. It doesn't matter what happened or why, it's one of the best gifts I've ever been given.

It happened like this.

It's 1991 and I'm in her apartment, living her third of our bicoastal relationship (one-third in New York, one-third in California, one-third apart), probably the only person in Manhattan looking forward to a summer in the city, when she says, "Honey, let's go to France."

I close my book and listen, petrified. I hate to fly and don't speak French. This isn't a good idea. I was in Paris in 1966, and they loathed me, and I don't think I've changed that much. "Let's go to Saskatchewan."

"It's not the same."

"I know. They speak English and we can drive."

"Don't worry. I'll take care of everything."

It's late May, a beautiful spring in New York, and this is her busiest time at work. As far as I can see, there's no need to start studying French.

That's my second mistake.

One week later, she announces she's found the perfect place. "It's special, magical, enchanted." She's a poet. Everything she says is exaggerated.

"Where?" I ask, thinking Paris, Nice, Cannes, Antibes.

"Brittany. It's as far west as you can go. Finistère."

"What does that mean?"

"The end of the world."

That's when I panic. I go to the bookstore and read in a guidebook that Bretons aren't French but Celtic—linked by language and culture to the Irish, Scots, Cornish, and Welsh—so maybe I do have a chance. On the other hand, they've been French since 1532, why chance it? I go to the Café des Artistes and write her a note. "Great work. Could you ask if the place is on-a-country-road quiet, sunny, and large? Does it have a good bed, hard mattress, running water, *hot* running water [remembering my stay in Paris], a TV, stereo, car, separate studies for writing, a coffeemaker, shower, bath, at least two floors, farm animals in the vicinity, a washing machine, dryer, and dishwasher, a bar in the village, a boulangerie, a market, a post office, bikes, and neighbors who want Americans living next door?" I leave it on her desk, thinking, Saskatchewan, here we come.

The next day she leaves me a message on her answering machine. "We have it—a thousand a month, with a car."

I wait a minute, put on my happy voice, and call her at work. "Hi . . . got your message."

"Ouiiiiiii," she sings.

"Does it have all those things I asked about?

"Certainement. The last thing I need is to listen to you complaining every day."

"It *really* has all those things?"

"That's what the lady said. Her name's Sally. She's English and just returned from the house. She lives in Massachusetts, you can ask her yourself."

So I do. I call her, and she says yes to everything. There's no way out. I'm going to France.

We book our flight on Air France. All I can think of is a joke I recently heard. "In Heaven, the French are the cooks, Italians are the lovers, English are the police, Swiss are the managers, and Germans are the engineers. In Hell, the English are the cooks, Swiss are the lovers, Italians are the engineers, Germans are the police, and the French are the managers." I know I'm going to die—but if I do, I'm going in comfort and style. The food on the flight is scrumptious, and we're flying economy. The meal begins with a printed menu and a choice of boeuf Bourguignon or filet de sole bonne femme. The wine is French—Côte du Rhône, Burgundy, Beaujolais—and is good and free and limitless. The front of the menu has a lovely little poem by La Fontaine. Mine is "Lion." Hers is "Swan." I look around and see four other poems. Everything about this is class. *Joie de vivre, savoir-faire, je ne sais quoi.* The movies, the nibbles and snacks, the pampering. If this is France, this is going to be all right, I think—until we get to the baggage claim, which brings me back to the joke.

The flight was wonderful, the landing superb. We took off and landed on time. The stewards and stewardesses were everything you'd want them to be in appearance, demeanor, humor, efficiency. I've slept. I'm full. I'm in Paris. I have everything I need—except my luggage. The good news is, nobody else has theirs either. The worst news is, an hour and a half later, it's still the same. Six and a half hours of relaxing comfort and pleasure getting here, and an hour and a half of standing up, nowhere to go, sit, eat, rest, drink, or relax.

It's baffling. Everything about Charles de Gaulle Airport is space-age, high-tech modern: tubes, lights, tunnels; escalators running up, down, sideways. The French love gadgets and gadgetry (think guillotine), and everything that can be is automated, everything except labor.

Two and a half hours later—9:30 on the dot—we're on the bus to Paris. We sit in the seat directly behind the driver. Kathryn takes the window and spends the next hour oohing and aaahing over the architecture and skyline. I spend it in awe of the driver, watching him alternately race to 130 kilometers per hour, then slow down to 30, only to race back to 130 and never once move more than eighteen inches away from the vehicle directly in front of us. He does this for fifty minutes, all the way from Charles de Gaulle Aéroport to downtown Paris, where he stops in front of a brasserie.

"Let's go," Kathryn says.

"Go where?"

"To the station."

For some reason—and I'm sure there is one, because there always is one, a reason, or rule, or *normalement*—the bus stop is across the street from the train station. Across *two* big busy streets in a city and a country not known for its kind, safe, considerate, California, pedestrian-has-the-right-of-way drivers. A phalanx of cars and trucks whizzes by and shakes the bus.

"Let's wait," I say.

"For what? This is the stop. Let's go." She pulls my hand.

I hesitate, then leap and run to the doorway of the brasserie to wait.

When everybody is off the bus and milling about, the driver pushes himself out of his seat, lumbers to the side of the bus, raises the panels, and lugubriously begins unloading the luggage. He does it with the seriousness and concentration of a brain surgeon. It's then that I notice his uniform bears no name. No "Hi, I'm Jacques, I'm your driver for the day." No "My name's Pierre. If I drive like a maniac or smash your bag, here's how you can report me." This bothers me, because in a second or two, whatever his name, he's going to hate us.

Everyone else's bags are relatively small and lightweight, but we're writers and staying for the summer. Between us we have nine heavy bags and two luggage carts. I have a computer. She has a typewriter. We each have a bag filled with books and another with files and notebooks and paper. She has lots and lots of shoes and clothes, something for any occasion. I have three bottles of twelve-year-old Macallan and a jacket and shoes for every kind of weather from blizzards and hurricanes to drought. The driver doesn't know any of this because someone else loaded the bags at the airport. Now, as he pulls them out, he begins to grumble. The fourth bag he yanks and drops on the sidewalk. The fifth he tosses at me. The sixth he throws. The seventh is Kathryn's typewriter. She taps him on the arm and tells him in flawless French that she's a poet and that's her typewriter and asks him to please be careful. He lifts it and puts it down gently, as gently as if it were a quail's egg, the last quail's egg in the world and he's the hungriest man alive. Then he starts talking to her about poetry, quoting Verlaine, Rimbaud, Baudelaire, and Poe, while I crawl into the luggage bin and tear my pants as I get my computer. When he finally finishes cooing and leaves, she's beaming. "La belle France, la belle France. *That's* why I love it here."

That's also when it starts to rain.

She unzips her backpack and removes an umbrella. I'm amazed and delighted by her forethought. My rain gear is all packed on the bottom of the one bag I have that isn't waterproof. I wait in grateful anticipation as she unsheathes her umbrella and opens it. It's Barbie's umbrella. Thumbelina's. The tiniest little umbrella in the universe. An umbrella for one. I wipe the water from my glasses and glare at her.

She shrugs.

I gather our bags as quickly as I can, balance and tie them to our luggage carts, and wait for a lull in the traffic. There is none. You'd think with the rain coming down harder and us standing there getting wet, someone might slow down. Not a chance. The morning Paris commute is a crazed Le Mans. I'm astonished. Can these be the same people who took two and a half hours to unload our bags?

Kathryn takes two steps into the street. I watch, as miraculously one car stops, then another, and another, and another. It's like royalty entering a room. The stillness is almost palpable. I follow in her wake through the traffic, across the streets, all the way into Gare Montparnasse, feeling unbeatable, like Napoleon must have felt just before Waterloo.

Gare Montparnasse is huge, gargantuan, signifying grandeur, power, control, direction, order, authority, a plan. The first floor, the one we're standing on, is a big wide-open space. In the middle of this space, slowly, inexorably, moving up and down, is a bank of escalators. On either side of the escalators are stairs.

I push my luggage cart around in ever-widening circles, looking for the elevator.

"What are you doing?"

"Looking for the elevator."

"I don't think there is one. I'll ask."

How can that be? This is a train station. A huge modern train station, the point of departure for all points west in France. How could old people, disabled people, people in wheelchairs, people carrying five heavy bags of luggage like me, get from this floor to the next without an elevator?

"Nope. No elevator. We have to take the escalator or the stairs."

"Ask someone else. A woman this time—an old one."

She glares at me, but she does it. She finds the oldest, crookedest person I've ever seen and returns shaking her head. "There is none. We have to use the escalator."

I glower at the old woman and watch to see what she does. I want to make sure she doesn't sneak off to some secret French person's elevator and leave the American to the escalator. She doesn't. She cautiously boards the escalator and white-knuckles the belt as it herky-jerks her upward, and I wonder for the first of many times: how can the French be so good at elegance and well-being, *joie de vivre* and *eau de vie* and *vie de vie*, and not have the slightest clue about ordinary, daily convenience—things like toilet seats, window screens, and shower curtains?

"Let's go," Kathryn calls, and wheels far away from me.

I follow and watch as three men open the line for her and make room for her and help her, while another holds her cart and bags in place with his knees. I wait for a break in the line, see none, and push my way in. Amazingly, no one complains or threatens to kill me.

I follow her to a fenced-in area, a square space roped off like a boxing ring, with a sign in the middle that says *Terrasse*. I know what that means: I'm going to pay more than the normal outrageous price for a cup of coffee the size of a thimble with no refill. She sits down and orders a café au lait and a brioche. I do the same by pointing at her, then at myself, and nodding my head up and down like a bobblehead. That's when I realize there are no sweatpants, track suits, or women in curlers. No beggars, homeless, or hungry people. No green hair or shaved heads, tattoos or pierced body parts—except for ears—and no crazies. *I'm* the scruffiest person on the *terrasse*, maybe even in the entire *gare*, Paris, and France. I look like an escapee from Devil's Island—rumpled, crumpled, pants torn from the bus, and sweaty. Everyone else looks like Saturday night at the ball. I look like Monday morning.

Our train is scheduled to depart at 1:05. I pay the bill—twenty dollars for two coffees and a basket of brioches—and we get up to amble and stretch, which turns out to be a mistake. At 12:00 virtually every French person not serving food in Gare Montparnasse stops whatever he or she is doing and starts to eat. By 12:05 not a single chair, table, bench, or horizontal surface is empty. There are lines—actually wedges, the French don't make lines—thirty and forty people deep waiting to buy a sandwich or a Coke or their ubiquitous bottle of water. Others are waiting in wedges just as deep for buffets. It's a regular feeding frenzy. At 11:55 we could have sat anywhere and bought anything. By 12:05 there's no place to go. I haven't seen anything like it since the piranha tank at the Brooklyn Aquarium.

The good news is while everyone is busy eating we can easily board the train. I locate the track and begin walking along it looking for our car.

"Wait, you have to post your ticket."

"What?"

"You have to post your ticket. It's not valid if you don't post it. It's a crime."

I walk back to where Kathryn's standing. "I thought these are reserved seats."

"They are."

"Then what's with this posting?"

"It's the law."

"How do you know? Where does it say? Where's the sign?" I've been in France five hours and already I'm gesticulating. "How is anyone supposed to know?"

She shrugs and points. I turn around and see another wedge of people standing in front of what looks like a time clock on an altar, which, given what they do with time, seems to me a sacrilege. I watch as, one by one, each person inserts his or her ticket into the machine, waits for it to click, then removes it, and goes on his or her validated way. They all look pleased with themselves, modern-day Saint Michaels, as if they've put their hand in the dragon's mouth and emerged with it unscathed. Then Kathryn does it too, and I follow her—again, and again, and again. It takes me three tries, as the ticket goes in only one way and there's no way on earth to know which way. I think about my father and his parents, Hungarians who emigrated to the U.S. from France, and my mother's parents, who emigrated from Hungary and Poland, all of them at Ellis Island, and about cultural differences and assumptions, the things we take for granted—like the subway system in New York, and how lucky I am I was born there and speak English, and that some of the people who work there do too.

It's in that mood that I search for our train car, not sure what to expect, French comfort or lack of convenience. It's a TGV bullet train, sleek and shiny, the Concorde of trains, but I've just come from the "modern airport," so I'm not expecting the best. I enter our car, look around, and relax. The seats are airline seats, *first-class airline seats*, leather, individually con-toured, with a headrest, footrest, and a table, and they recline. The windows are huge and spotless. The lights are bright, and the bathroom smells good and works. The train, like the plane, is wonderful, and like the plane, it departs on time. At precisely 1:05, we leave Gare Montparnasse and head west for Brittany, Finistère—the end of the world.

I take out my book, Céline's *Journey to the End of the Night*, and start reading. This is my summer for French lit. Along with everything else, I'm carrying Stendhal, Proust, Flaubert, Hugo, Balzac, Sartre, Camus, Voltaire, Maupassant, Bataille, Sarraute, and Réage. Kathryn is carrying the poets and read-ing Baudelaire—in French. Our plan is to sit for a while, read, look out the window, and buy lunch on the train when we feel like it.

Ten minutes out of the station, everyone, as if on cue, starts removing food from bags, boxes, sacks, purses, coats, scarves, pockets, day packs, backpacks, suitcases, socks, you name it: breads of every size and shape; sausages; cheeses that are round, square, wedged, rolled, and rectangular, white, gray, black, blue, green, and yellow, with aromas that go from sweet honey to bathroom; there's fruit, casseroles, chicken, choco-late, crêpes, crackers, chips, and liters and liters of water: Evian, Vittel, Volvic, Isabelle, Perrier, Badoit, Vichy. In no time at all everyone is eating, except us.

The sight of us sitting there without any food must have been too much for them. The woman in the aisle seat next to me reaches over and hands me a hunk of bread and a slab of sausage.

"Merci," I say. For me, it's the end of the conversation. For her, it's the start. She speaks rapidly. I nod and nod and say a few "ouis" and hope she will quit, but she doesn't.

Kathryn switches seats with me and speaks with her and translates. "The bread is a multigrain, made the old way in a brick oven by an artisan. The sausage is an andouille. It comes from her brother's farm near Saint-Brieuc."

Upon hearing her speak French and understand it, everyone around us joins in, first by giving us more things to eat, then by telling us what we are eating, where it comes from, how it's made, the ingredients, locations, specialties, what's homegrown, homemade, artisan-made, natural, fresh.

The conversation switches back and forth from the serious—food, family, the land, weather—to the hilarious: what kind of water to buy; no sodium, too much sodium, not enough sodium, carbonated, noncarbonated, flavored, natural. At one point I think a Badoit person is going to bean a Vittel. There's lots of "offs" and "bawees" and laughter, and a strange sucking noise that sounds to me like the whistle of an incoming aerial bomb.

About an hour and a half out of Paris the woman sitting directly in front of me, who has yet to say a word to us, turns around and asks, "Vous habitez en Angleterre?" You're from England?

"Non. Nous sommes américains."

Everything changes after that. I expect to have to duck and cover and answer questions like, Why is your country ruining the Earth? Instead they ask about us, where we live in the United States, how long we'll be in France, why we're going to Brittany and Finistère, and what we're going to do there. When Kathryn tells them we're writers, that we've come to visit and write, they all make that sharp sucking sound and say, "Bien sûr," as if it were preordained. The woman sitting behind me then says something about Chateaubriand. The fellow next to her, a round portly gent with a nose the color of eggplant, says, "Non, non, non," and goes on and on about Max Jacob and Jules Verne. The woman who first gave me the bread and sausage stops him, points to my book, and tells us to go to Camaret, where Céline lived out the final years of his miserable life. At the mention of Camaret, a man dressed in blue-and-green plaid pants and a green-and-blue striped shirt, and who doesn't look half bad, takes a harmonica out of his jacket pocket and begins to play "The girls from Camaret," a little local ditty like "Mademoiselle from Armentières," and follows it up with some down-home James Carter Chicago blues.

The closer we get to Brest, the more jovial everyone becomes. More food is passed around, foods we hadn't seen earlier, pastries and cakes with Breton names: *kouign amann*, *far Breton*, and *galettes* from Pont-Aven that make Danish butter cookies taste as if they're made with lard. There's cider and wine and more conversation about local specialties—oysters, crab, mussels, langoustine, salmon, monkfish, and what else to see and do in Brittany. Just before we arrive at the station, a boy, maybe thirteen or fourteen, comes over and shyly asks in broken English if Kathryn would write a note in English to a girl he met in Dublin the previous summer. She does, of course, and when she gives it to him and wishes him "bonne chance," he blushes and thanks us and kisses us both on each cheek. Everyone around us hoots and whistles and claps.

As the train pulls into the station, people begin saying their good-byes—*au revoir, bonne journée, à bientôt*. Clearly, this is important to them, this business of getting together and leaving. They say their good-byes cheerfully and with smiles but also with a sense of loss. It was the same with the stewards and stewardesses at Charles de Gaulle when they said their *au revoirs* as we deplaned. They said it as if they meant it, as if something significant had happened between us. And, as if to make that point, the woman who first gave me the sausage and bread comes over to me, shakes my hand, kisses me twice, once on each cheek, and pats my arm. I stand there and wave bye-bye.

We have an hour's wait for the commuter train that will take us to our village. Kathryn goes to the office to buy our tickets. I push and pull the luggage carts into the station and look for a place to leave them. There is none. No Baggage Claim. No Left Luggage. Zip. On my third or fourth circle around the station, I find a bank of about ten lockers that are camouflaged to look like the wall, none larger than a bread box. All of them are locked, in use. It's extraordinary, really, the number of ways France finds to make daily life a difficulty. I look around for a bench to sit on. None of those either. Not a chair or a seat, unless you count the floor, which several people are already using. It's just like the airport while we waited for our baggage.

I push and pull the carts outside and wait. Except for the signs in French, the station and everything around it is Anywhere, U.S.A., 1950s–'60s postwar, ugly, cheap. I studied European history in college and know a little about France and the war. Brittany was occupied by the Germans, and Brest, which had been one of the chief naval ports in France for centuries, served the same function for Germany. The Germans based the submarines they used in the Battle of the Atlantic here, and the *Bismarck* was heading here when it was sunk. Brest was liberated by the U.S. Army under Patton in 1944, and in the process was completely destroyed by the constant bombardments and house-to-house, hand-to-hand combat. That's why it looks like Newark.

I leave the luggage—something I'd never do in the U.S.—and cross the street to look at the bay. Bright yellow cranes unload a red-and-green tanker. Sailboats of all sizes and shapes—including three old tall masters with rust-orange sails, painted rowboats, barges, yachts, trawlers, ferries, even a kayak and a racing scull—move in and out and around the harbor. It's a lovely, tranquil sight: bright yellow cranes, primary-colored boats, white cotton candy clouds, silvery light, and the blue-green sea. I try to imagine what it was like before the war, and during the war, and how beautiful and awful it must have been.

I return to the station and find Kathryn. We go to the track, and this time I manage to post my ticket correctly on the second attempt and board the local commuter train, which is like the Toonerville Trolley, two little green cars with tiny baggage compartments. As before, the people are reticent, but also as before, become friendly and funny and curious. One woman wants to know where we're from, another where we're going, and all want to know why we're there. Kathryn, in her perfectly accented and conjugated French, explains.

I nod while she tells them, periodically say "Oui," and shrug, while stealing glances through the windows at the lush, verdant land, a quilt of greens, tiny squares, rectangles, and triangles divided and subdivided by rows of hedges, stunted trees, and stone walls. The land is hilly, roly-poly, looking beautiful, wintry in the early evening mist, and hard to sow. Cows and sheep graze everywhere. I don't see a single person, but dotting the land like punctuation are huge rolls of hay and small, two-story stone houses with dark slate roofs. There's a fixedness to it all that's comforting.

We arrive in Loscoat forty minutes later, where a taxi is waiting at the station. On the ride to the house, Kathryn once again explains who we are, where we're from, and why we're there, as I oooh and aah over the shops in the village—*bou-langerie, pâtisserie, crêperie, charcuterie*—the old stone bridge we drive over, the river, sailboats, people fishing along the quay, the flowers—bright red geraniums and fuchsias perched on windowsills and hanging from lampposts, pink, white, and blue hydrangeas lining the road—the sky, and that light again, even with the clouds, the vitality and durability of everything, including the old men playing *boules* and finally our village, Plobien, a one-road hamlet with a row of three-story stucco houses and an occasional stand-alone house facing the river, and our house, Chez Sally: a blue-shuttered, white stucco row house thirty feet from the quay. As we step out of the cab, the driver points up. A double rainbow dusts the sky. The three of us watch until it fades and disappears. Then the driver leaves and Kathryn goes next door to get the keys from our contact, a Madame Piriou, the person who will change my life.

I sit on the steps and look at the river. On the other side is a crumbled old stone house with broken-down walls that once must have been a château. Around it are open fields where cows graze and horses run wild. A fish leaps out of the water and lands gracelessly with a flop. From upriver—or down, I can't tell—a sailboat heads my way. It doesn't get any more perfect than this. I take Céline from my backpack and start to read. I'm expecting to wait fifteen or thirty minutes because nothing in France, except the driving, seems to go fast. Kathryn returns in a paragraph, a *Céline paragraph*, which surprises, pleases, and bothers me. I don't know what it means, but I know it means something. This is France, and every human thing does.

I put the key in the lock and fiddle with it and finally open the door. Dankness engulfs us, followed by a funeral smell.

"It's an old stone house," Kathryn says. "It's normal—C'est *normal*," a phrase I would learn to hate.

I pull the bags in and leave them in the hallway. I also leave the door open to let in the light and out the smell.

"Look, a stereo, TV, VCR, and dozens of English and American movies on tape." I follow her voice, with a mixture of hope and dread, into the combined living room–dining room. The windows are shuttered so I can't see out. There are a table and four chairs for eating and a couch and three chairs for sitting, all pretty ratty looking, which is fine with me: nothing here to destroy.

"There's a dishwasher, clothes washer, and dryer, in the kitchen." I peek in and see that they, along with the stove and refrigerator, are Whirlpool, Philips, and Brandt, American, Dutch, and German. For some reason that reassures me.

We go upstairs to the second floor, which the French call the first floor, *le premier étage*, and find a small study at the top of the stairwell. The window is unshuttered and looks out at the river, the hills and fields, and the sky, an encouraging sight. It's a little nest, this room, with its writing desk, captain's chair, and three-shelf bookcase filled with English and American books. Kathryn looks at me and I look at her, and we smile, knowing this is going to be a fight: Who's going to get this room? We leave it as fast as we can.

I push open the door to the adjoining room and enter the bedroom. It's big and airy and has an even larger window than the study and lets in the same view, only more of it, and oodles and oodles of light. Everything glimmers, including the dust and the spiderwebs. I sit on the double bed facing the mirrored armoire and watch myself bounce up and down. Then I lie down and roll over and over again. "The mattress is firm," I pronounce.

"That's what the lady said," Kathryn says, as she disappears into the bathroom. I follow her. It has a shower, thank God, and a bidet—something I yearn to use. The toilet's in a separate room—a great idea, right up there with evolution, and probably responsible for saving thousands of relationships.

On the third floor, *le deuxième étage*, there's another bedroom with a double bed that isn't so firm (I find out later that summer), a tiny sitting room with a torn sofa, a scuzzy sink and toilet, and, to my great relief, another study. It has the same view as the first one, and it's a little larger, has a bigger desk, a leather chair, more books, and a radio. I can't believe our luck. The house has two studies on three floors—a floor for each of us to work on: the third for me; the second for her. "You did it," I say, giving her a hug and a kiss. "Nice work."

"Thanks," she says. "I'm beat."

It's nine o'clock in the evening and still as light as if it were three in the afternoon. We've been traveling twenty hours, door to door. I follow her down the stairs to the second-floor bedroom, on *le premier étage*, where she lies fully clothed on the bed. I continue down the stairs to close and lock the door. Then I go back to the bedroom, open the window, and lie down next to her and fall asleep. Sometime in the early-morning hours I wake up, then she does too, and we lie there in the light of the moon as the breeze from the river washes over us. The last thing she says before I fall asleep is "Bienvenue en France."

"Merci," I say, and mean it, and I still do. *Merci, merci.*

Over the next two months we drive each other crazy and fall out of love, and in spite of that, or to spite that, or despite that, or having nothing at all to do with that, I begin to fall in love with Brittany, Finistère, the end of the world.

There

I wake to the sounds of a whining, screeching, squeaking, pleading piece of machinery making its way slowly down the road, followed by the pealing of church bells, again and again and again and again. Some type A farmer, I figure, out getting his worm. I roll over and go back to sleep. The buzz of a motorbike wakes me. The church bells chime. I look at the clock. It's 5:30.

I get up and look out the window. One story down is the two-lane country road we arrived on last night. On the other side of the road is the river, about fifty feet wide at that point, and on the other side of the river are a dilapidated stone wall and building. Beyond the ruins the dark outline of the hills flow like waves.

I put on the jeans and shirt I wore yesterday, not bothering to shower, brush my teeth, or comb my hair. Who am I going to offend at five-thirty? I tiptoe down the stairs and turn the key I left in the lock. Nothing. I turn the key the other way, clockwise, thinking maybe the French do it backward, like calling the second floor the first. More nothing. I pull the key out, examine it for I don't know what, put it back in, and turn it. Zero. I turn it upside-down—it won't go in. I put it back in the right way, turn it left, right, back and forth. Nothing. Nothing. Nothing. There's no way to open the door. I'm stuck. I go into the living room to stew.

The church bells chime, bong, bong, bong, six times. I've been up for half an hour and haven't done a thing—already I'm becoming more French. I pull open the window, which opens inward, and unlatch the shutters, which open out, and watch the sun rise over the hills. As the light touches the water, the surface mists and fogs. It could be the set for a horror movie—*Deliverance, Night of the Living Dead*, or *The War of the Roses*—only it's not scary, it's magical, enchanting, serene. I want to go out.

I sit on the windowsill, spin around with my legs facing out, and jump—almost landing on a woman walking by. She has a baguette in one hand and a dog's leash in the other. I look at the dog. It looks like a rat with hair. The baguette looks like a baguette. The woman doesn't say anything, she doesn't even blanch—as if this is the way French people leave their houses every day, or at least the way English people do, because clearly I'm not French and this is the house of the English lady.

I point to her bread and nod my head up and down like a yo-yo. The lady squeezes the bread to her breasts and reels in the dog.

"Où," I say, "Où . . . où est le pan?" As soon as I say it I realize what I said is, "Où est lapin," "Where, where, where is the bunny?"

Without blinking or laughing or wasting a single word on someone to whom it would clearly be lost, she turns around and points with her baguette.

"Merci," I say, but she's too far away to hear me.

I cross the street and walk on the path next to the river. Hydrangeas the size of bowling balls bloom in reds, blues, pinks, and whites. Two swans emerge from the mist like U-boats and home in on a bucket of bread that someone, perhaps the baguette lady, left for them on the quay. A heron stands watch on the other side of the river, and black-and-white magpies do what they do, with a little too much glee, it seems to me.

I walk in the direction the baguette pointed. Sunlight ricochets off the water onto the front of the houses, tickling the quartz in the granite and making it twinkle. The shutters are all closed. Everybody except the insomniacs, baguette lady, and I seems to be asleep. It's idyllic, a fairyland—a land of make-believe. . . . No kidding!

I stop when I see the street sign—Place du Général de Gaulle—and marvel once again at France's willingness and ability to rewrite its history. Why else have two empires, five republics, and a revolution that not only changed the government but the names of the days, months, and years? I remember from my first visit that every village, city, town, and crossroads had its Place Charles de Gaulle or Place de la Résistance or Rue Jean Moulin or Jean Juares or Général LeClerc, as if everyone in France had the same history, had been a member of the Free French Army or the Maquis, and everyone was antifascist and no one had collaborated, and neither Vichy nor Drancy existed.

I look around. The *place* has all of the requisite buildings—a church, *mairie*, *poste*, and their faithful companions, a bar and a bar-tabac. The bar is closed, but the bar-tabac is open and full. Three old guys are starting their day or ending their day or don't know the difference between night and day, sitting at a table with three tiny glasses and a big bottle of red. On the other side of the *place*, where the main road turns inland, is an insurance office, and next to that is the *boulangerie*. A single-lane road continues paralleling the river and, according to the sign, leads to a *pâtisserie*, a viaduct, and a restaurant. That's it, my village, the village I'm going to be living in for the next eight weeks, smaller than a small-town suburban mall.

I walk to the fountain in the center. It looks as if it's been a long time without water, which is odd, since this is Brittany, and it's supposed to rain all the time. The front of the *mairie*—city hall—is pockmarked and peeling. Chimneys are in need of repair—some are broken, others have become planters with grass and weeds growing out of them. Three of the buildings look completely unoccupied, and the church, the largest and probably oldest building, is black from base to bell tower, covered with soot or dirt or exhaust.

The church door swings open and two women come out, and just like the baguette lady, neither of them looks at me. I'm invisible, which, given how I look, *is* a miracle. If *I* saw me, I would stare.

"Bonjour," I say as I walk up the steps.

"Bonjour, monsieur," they respond in harmony.

I walk in expecting medieval doom and gloom, and am surprised by the airiness and light. The ceiling is the blue of the bluest summer sky I can imagine, the walls white like clouds. I walk down the aisle between newly caned, squat-legged, straight-backed, neatly arranged rows of painfully uncomfortable-looking chairs. No sissy cushions, benches, or kneelers for these people. Also, no Jesus or cross on the altar. It's not until I reach the front railing that I see Him hanging there, a little ten-inch guy made of bronze. I've had enough Irish and Italian girlfriends to know it isn't like this in Catholic churches in America. In the U.S., there's always a Jesus on the altar. A big, dominating, conquering, possessing Jesus. *This* guy looks like a shrimp. I don't get it. I turn around to leave and see Him—the Big One—hanging on the inside of one of the stone arches as if He's embarrassed by all the fuss and trying to be inconspicuous. What isn't inconspicuous are the lavishly embroidered gold-silver-ruby-emerald-sapphire-colored banners for Saint Anne, Saint Thérèse, Mary, and Joan of Arc that line the walls. No wonder the U.S. and France so often disagree. The U.S. celebrates Peter, Paul, Patrick, and John, the manly saints, and France is a girlie state. As I'm leaving, I spot a tiny altar off to my left with more lit candles on it than the altar in front.

It's a statue of a woman—of course!—a cameo standing in an oval niche. The niche is painted a brighter version of the bluest summer sky and matches the color of her eyes. It reminds me of those dioramas in the natural history museum in New York, only what's made three-dimensional here isn't the physical but the ethereal—fine, powdery, *heavenly* clouds emanating from behind her, levitating in the blue sky. She's wearing a black robe and holding a crucifix, looking into the sky, not blissfully, but humanly, waiting for and wanting something she knows she's not going to get. It's six o'clock in the morning, and she's surrounded by lit candles, fresh flowers, and marble plaques that say *Merci.* There's something terrible and comforting about her. Next to her, I see, is her card. *I* don't have a card, but here even the dead saints do. I take one. It says *Sainte Rita Avocate des Causes Désespérées* and beneath it, *Sainte Rita Priez pour nous.* I hope so. I surely do, because I'm going to need all the help I can get. I say good-bye to Saint Rita and wish her a happy day, though given what she's the saint of, it probably isn't going to happen too soon.

The bells chime once as I leave the church. There's nothing to do except join the old guys in the bar-tabac or buy my daily bread. I cross the street and push the *boulangerie* door. It doesn't budge. I push again, harder. It still doesn't budge. I look inside. There are people there, and the lady on the street had her baguette. It has to be open. I push again. *Merde.* Another French door that doesn't work. What is it with this country? An old lady in a blinding floral dress and a handbag the size of a suitcase points at something written above the handle. *Tirez.* I push. She pulls. That's it—I'm a pusher, and France is a nation of pullers. It's a lesson I'll have to learn.

"Merci," I say, as I step into the store. Seven people are waiting ahead of me, in a wedge. In the U.S. it would look like a stakeout or some kind of takeover. In Brittany, it's French people waiting for bread. Even more amazing is how they're dressed: the women in skirts and pumps with sweaters and scarves; the men in slacks, shirts with collars, and shiny shoes. No pajamas, bathrobes, hair curlers, jogging outfits, or sweatpants on anyone. In my torn pants and yesterday's T-shirt, with uncombed hair, unshaven, and unwashed, no one in the shop looks like me. No one looks *at* me either. In the U.S., if someone like me came into a small shop everyone would stare, fuss, become very quiet or very loud, and pretend I didn't exist. Here, I really don't.

The baker, a young man in his late twenties or early thirties wearing a spotless white apron, his black hair and mustache covered with flour—no hair nets here!—greets each person as he or she steps forward from his or her place in the wedge. "Bonjour. Ça va?" Hello, how's it going? It's enough to get the conversation started. I've seen it before. There could be a hundred people in that wedge, and each person will get the time to say whatever it is he or she needs to say. In New

York, at six in the morning, with half a dozen tired, hungry people in line behind you, you and the baker would be dead for taking so much as a millisecond longer than the actual exchange required. If you waited in line and didn't know what you wanted when your turn came or didn't have your money ready to pay on the spot, God help you. None of which seems to matter here.

People who have been buying bread in this shop for years, who have the same selection to choose from every day, take minutes to decide what they want. People who know the price of every item down to the centime act as if it's the first time they've heard the price and spend minutes counting out their change. No one fidgets. No one gets angry. Everyone is talking to someone: the first person in line to the baker, and everyone else to each another. Except to me.

Thankfully, they leave me alone. I look around, trying to find what I want. I see croissants in a case behind the counter. Milk is in the refrig—*in bottles*. I take one. There's no way to know if it's low-fat, skim, or whole, and for me no way to ask. I just hope I don't have buttermilk. Jam, *confiture*, is on a shelf. I take one jar of apricot and one of strawberry. I also take a package of coffee, *café*. The only thing I don't see is sugar—and I don't know how to ask for it. I'm looking for it when I suddenly realize nobody else is holding any merchandise in their hands, and that maybe this isn't self-serve. I watch, but I can't tell. Everyone else just gets bread, which is stacked behind the baker against the wall. I'm not sure what to do—hold what I have or put it back?

I watch as an old lady with spindly legs, a great big chignon, and a husky, vibrant laugh buys three large loaves of something and proceeds to count out a zillion tiny coins. When she's finished she asks for something else and the baker walks around the counter to get it for her. While she's paying for *that* with another zillion coins, I put the milk, jam, and coffee back where I found them and wait my turn to ask. I know *fromage*, *café*, *confiture*, *baguette*, and *croissant*. I don't know the word for milk, but I know cow from Happy Cow cheese, La Vache Qui Rit, and I knew juice, *jus*.

The good news is the wedge moves slowly, so I have plenty of time to practice. The bad news is a century would have been too short. My thinking goes like this. I'll say "Bonjour, monsieur." Then he'll say something, I'll nod and smile and shrug and say "Oui. Une baguette, deux croissants, fromage, confiture, café, et jus du vache, s'il vous plaît." Amazingly, it actually goes that way. He scoops everything up and says something I know is a number and haven't a clue. I make a writing motion with my hand, as in Write it for me, *s'il vous plaît?* He writes 60,35: 60 francs and 35 centimes, a little over ten dollars, a fair price if I had money, which I don't. I didn't expect to go shopping at five-thirty in the morning when I jumped out the window.

Now I get to do my version of Marcel Marceau. I turn my palms up and shrug. I put my hands in my pockets and shrug. I turn my pockets inside out and shrug. I point out the window to where I think the house is and say "Mon ami," then put my hands together, hold them to my cheek, and tilt my head sideways to indicate I have a friend somewhere out there who is sleeping or dead.

Finally someone in the wedge behind me gets tired of the show and says something. The only word I understand is "Anglais," English. That seems to be enough of an explanation for everyone, and they all say "Ah oui, ah oui" repeatedly.

The baker bags everything for me and sends me on my way with a "Bonne journée." I almost say the same to him, but it's

6:00 a.m. and he's been up for hours baking bread, and he'll be working for hours more, and he probably isn't going anywhere, so wishing him a good trip, a good journey, would be rude and inconsiderate. So I wave and say "Oui" and leave. How am I supposed to know *bonne journée* means "have a good day"?

Outside, I'm relieved and amazed. How do these people stay in business? For a people who gave us the words *bourgeois* and *entrepreneur*, it's strange behavior.

I wait for a truck filled with little piggies who definitely are going to market to pass before I cross the street. The sun is up, and the river is sparkling. A family of ducks float by. A man in a sailboat calls, "Bonjour." I wave and that's when I see him, the World War I infantryman standing under a tree next to the public showers and bath looking heavenward, forlorn and lost. I don't have to read the inscription beneath him to know what it says: *À ses enfants morts pour la France.*

I stop and count the names. Fifty-two, three of them from one family, the Pennecs. Ten percent of the village—twenty percent of the men—*killed*. Add the maimed and the broken and the ruined, and you reach the standard figure of one-third: thirty-three percent of all of the men in France killed or maimed in the First World War. Behind the statue, on the back, facing the river, are twenty names from World War II, including three more Pennecs. I know the English still disparage the French for surrendering in 1940, but it was Neville Chamberlain who cut the deal that set the fate. The war might very well have been England's finest hour, the prewar definitely was not. Meanwhile, the French and English continue their thousand-year mutual unadmiration society. In England, a prophylactic is called a French letter. In France, it's an English cap.

I walk back to the house, climb through the open window, and find Kathryn sitting in the living room, crying.

"What's the matter?"

"I'm sorry, I'm so sorry," she says.

I love hearing those words, even if I don't know what they're for. Eventually, I ask.

"This place. This house. Everything."

"It's fine. I like it here."

"Look," she says, pulling me into the kitchen.

Dirty dishes fill the sink.

"So we'll wash them. Big deal."

She opens the oven. It has dark, black, crispy tumorlike things growing from all six sides. I blanch. "Okay, so we won't bake."

She opens the fridge. I slam it shut. One whiff is enough to kill, one nanosecond enough to ruin the air. Inside, something is dead. Bird carcass, fish, rabbit, something foul, not to mention a horrible green. She walks me through. Dirty sheets, towels, and women's clothes fill the clothes hamper. The dryer, which may or may not work, has damp, moldy clothes in it. The washing machine is full. There are open boxes of food in the cupboards. The one closet is stale and scummy. I turn on the light to see more and watch the bulb flicker, twitch, then pop.

"What's that?" I ask, pointing to a gadget over the sink about the size of a cereal box—the regular size, not the giant.

"The water heater."

"You're kidding." I turn it on and it makes an impressive noise, a noise that means business, like a jet breaking the sound barrier. It takes two minutes to heat up. The hot water lasts about forty-five seconds before it runs out.

Kathryn yanks open the cabinet doors. I slide my thumb

over a plate and leave a skid mark an inch wide. The cups are chipped and caked, the glassware opaque. I open the silverware drawer and see encrusted food on the serving spoons and something brown on a fork.

I find another lightbulb—a 40-watter—and twist it in. I see food splotches in a paisley pattern on the floor and walls and spiderwebs in every corner, nook, and cranny, including the ceiling, before the bulb pops.

That's the kitchen. Every room is its own disaster, each with its own surprise. I had no idea there were so many different shades of green and brown. The rugs have grit in them, the walls mold. Bugs are everywhere—an entomologist's delight: ants, bees, wasps, flies, mosquitoes, crawly things. The floors are alive, and it isn't with the sound of music, or at least not the kind of music I want to hear.

The toilet is filthy, the shower greasy. There's hair on the walls, the floor, the drain, the soap. Above the showerhead is another of those cereal-size boxes. I know what that means: forty-five-second showers.

Kathryn starts to cry again. I take her hand, lead her down the stairs, and sit her in front of the open window. "Look at the river and the boats and the sky."

I peel the tablecloth from the table, leaving a swatch of fibers behind. I open four *New Yorkers*: one for Kathryn, one for me, and two for the food. I place the cheese, jam, milk, and croissants on the two *New Yorkers*, being careful to balance the baguette on top of the jam and the milk so it doesn't touch the table. I find a saucepan that isn't as greasy or moldy or encrusted as the others, and doesn't have aluminum peeling from its bottom, wash it, and fill it with water, which I intend to boil for a long time. I turn the knob and the pilot catches, sputters, and burns a bright orange flame. I find two cups that look salvageable and turn on the water, wait two minutes for it to heat, and then use my forty-five seconds to scald my hands and wash the cups with a bar of bath soap. I rinse them with the jolt of cold water that follows. I'm definitely not looking forward to bathing.

While waiting for the water to boil, I remember something a tour guide said when I visited Chenonceau. She said the French decided having running water in a house was unhygienic. A thousand years earlier the Romans knew about fresh water and aqueducts and how to bring water into the home, but the French thought dirty water, filthy water, *sewer* water with human waste, offal, and worse flowing through the house, *sitting* in the house, was wrong. They opted for no running water or indoor plumbing when they built their châteaux, homes, and apartments, choosing hand-filled baths and chamber pots instead, and this is the result: conveniences that are add-ons, coming years after the houses were built, often not until the 1950s. Hence, heating that only heats if you sit directly in front of the heater and only heats the side that's facing it, water heaters the size of cereal boxes, showers that trickle, hole-in-the-floor toilets, and electricity that flickers and pops. No wonder they invented perfume and eau de toilette.

"Okay," I say, "Let's eat." We sit in shimmering light, facing the open window, looking at the river, wheat-covered hills, and marshmallow sky. A man walks past without looking in, the most amazing thing I've seen so far. I can't pass an open anything without peeking. It illustrates a restraint and respect for privacy that's beyond me.

The church bells chime seven times. We eat slowly, knowing what's next. When we finish, we search the house for cleaning supplies. There's a broken broom, a vacuum cleaner without bags, no soap besides bar soap, no detergent, no mop, and no gloves—and neither one of us is going to touch anything without gloves—no sponges, no paper towels, and no rags, unless you count what's in the dryer and washer. Kathryn calls Sally to complain. She apologizes, says she left in a hurry, and will refund a week's rent. After that, there's only one thing to do—go to Madame P, the keeper of the keys.

Kathryn knocks on the door. Madame answers. Monsieur stands behind her, looking around her. A dog stands behind him, barking. The dog looks like something from *Sesame Street*, with hair completely covering his eyes. Madame says "Oui," and stands there, a fortress, waiting. She's completely dressed, as is Monsieur, and both look like they're expecting us for dinner. She's wearing a bright-patterned dress, a complementary scarf, and low heels. She's perfectly coiffed and her skin is like peaches and cream. Monsieur is as tan as if he lived in Tahiti. He's wearing dark pressed slacks, a green Lacoste shirt, and he's smoking. *I'm* wearing what I wore yesterday, and Madame is not impressed. Our only hope is Kathryn.

In great, great detail Kathryn describes the house, the filth, *le désastre*. In English, when she speaks in superlatives it drives me nuts. In French, superlatives are the way to go. The more Kathryn says, the more Madame listens. Occasionally she makes that sucking sound that sounds like incoming. Monsieur steps forward and does it once, too. The dog stops barking and listens. Kathryn walks them room by room through *les dommages*—the damage, the pity, the shame.

The more Kathryn tells her, the happier Madame gets. "Oui, oui." She smiles like a madwoman. From out of our depths and despair she becomes one of the happiest people alive. Monsieur, too. With the dog, it's hard to tell.

Finally, when Kathryn's done, Madame says something, finishes with "À bientôt," and waves us away.

As far as I can tell, "À bientôt" is our only hope. "Now what?"

"We wait."

"For what?"

"Madame."

"For what?"

"I think she's going to help."

"Help" is only a euphemism for what Madame and Monsieur provide. In less than twenty minutes, they're knocking on the door. I open it, and Madame looks at me, disappointed. I look at her, dumbfounded. She and Monsieur, between them, have enough cleaning supplies to clean the Love Canal. I call Kathryn and Madame smiles. Clearly, Kathryn has won her over. I, however, am another story. Madame and Monsieur dump all of their stuff in the hallway and then go home for more. It's amazing. How one family could even have so many cleaning supplies is beyond me. And why?

Madame shows us. There's a special broom for the tile of the kitchen floor, another for the wood in the living room, and another for the linoleum in the bathroom. There are three different mops as well. There are also different cleaning supplies for each type of floor as well as for drinking glasses, windows, dishes, silverware, the stove, the oven, counters, cabinets, the walls, the shower, the bathroom, the toilet, the sink. She and Monsieur are a team. She calls for an item, he hands it to her, and she demonstrates, careful to make sure she doesn't actually touch anything herself. After demonstrating each item, where and how it is to be used, Madame looks at me and shakes her head.

On their third trip, they carry a vacuum cleaner, lots of vacuum bags, garbage bags, two packages of paper towels, each containing twelve rolls, sponges, plastic gloves, a scraper, steel wool, laundry detergent, bleach, and several buckets. It's hard to believe so many different products could exist and be used, as opposed to, say, Ajax. What I'm learning here are two facts of French life: (1) the propensity for cleanliness. In the U.S., cleanliness is next to godliness. In France, it *is* godliness; and (2) the deeply held faith in specialization. In France, there's a product for everything—just as there is a worker for everything. One does not hire a general contractor. One hires a plumber, an electrician, a carpenter, a person for the heater, the roof, the floors, the windows, the door, the gate, the terrace, etcetera. Each person is specially trained and certified. The same holds true for doctors and auto mechanics: *spécialistes*. After all, if a product cleans a floor, how could it possibly clean a counter? If it cleans a counter, how could it clean a stove, a toilet, a sink? So here I am, surrounded by a zillion supplies and implements and a beaming Madame, Monsieur, and their dog. They leave with a smile and an "Au revoir," neither of which makes me happy.

The plan is simple. We'll approach it like Normandy. The first thing we need is beachhead. The kitchen is the place. The refrigerator is Omaha, and mine. Kathryn will take Juno, the cabinets and the sink. Neither of us mentions the oven, though my plan is to boil and stir-fry all summer. I have no idea what Kathryn plans, but I know it won't be good for me.

The first thing I do is scour four pots so we can boil water on the stove because the two-minute wait for forty-five-second hot-water heater is death. If we rely on that, we'll be cleaning well into the end of the third millennium—and that's an optimistic projection. We keep the water boiling and refill the pots. If this is war, we are *M*A*S*H*.

It takes all morning to clean the refrigerator. Even the ice cubes are dirty. I pull my T-shirt over my nose and make my way through, shelf by shelf, wall by wall, wiping and scraping out gunk that's so far past its prime it isn't even possible to determine what it began as: solid or liquid; salad or dessert; meat, fish, or fowl; animal, vegetable, or fruit. Talk about the mystery of life!

Meanwhile, Kathryn cleans the dishes, cups, glasses, and silverware: everything that is out and dirty; plus everything that's in the cabinets and just as dirty. She cleans every single utensil, then lays out rows of paper towels five layers thick to serve as shelf paper before putting everything back.

At 12:30 I sit down in the living room, hungry and thinking about lunch. I'm about to ask Kathryn what she wants to do, when Madame comes in carrying more bundles. "Déjeuner," she says, "déjeuner." I think it's more cleaning supplies, something especially designed for breakfast.

She sees Kathryn working in the kitchen and me sitting down and shakes her head sadly but definitely not in surprise. She clears off the dining room table, waving me away when I stand to help, and covers it with her own clean tablecloth, then places two plates, glasses, knives, forks, and spoons on the table along with sugar, butter, honey, three kinds of her homemade jam, and a large bottle of Vichy water. I'm hoping this makes her a collaborator with us.

"Mangez, mangez," she orders, and like a magician, pulls a tinfoil-covered plate from her basket and uncovers it. On it is a two-inch pile of crêpes. I'm so hungry and thankful I want to hug her, but I know if I do, she'll deck me.

"Merci," I keep saying, "Merci, merci, merci beaucoup." Kathryn kisses her four times, twice on each cheek. I shake her hand, then she leaves, and we sit at the table and eat. The crêpes are warm and chewy. The butter melts into them and infuses them, and when sugar, honey, or jam are added, they become breakfast and dessert in one: comfort and extravaganza. I'm hooked—on crêpes and the view from the window.

Three swans float lazily past. It's so bright you'd think they'd need sunglasses. A girl paddles lazily in a rubber raft. On the hillside across the road cows munch away, happily oblivious to what's next. Horses snooze. A salmon leaps out of the water. A tractor starts up. It's a perfect interlude, the promise of life to come, if we don't die of the plague.

"Bonjour," Madame calls as she knocks and pushes open the door. She's carrying a huge bouquet of mixed hydrangeas—red, pink, blue, white, and purple. She surveys the table, sees all the crêpes are gone, smiles, and says "Ahhhhh-hhhhh" in a lilt going up three octaves. She holds the flowers out for Kathryn. "Pour vous. Pour la maison propre." Pour moi, there's that look—like what besides *that* can you do?

I try to show her. I pick up the dishes, glasses, and silverware and start to carry them into the kitchen. Madame grabs my arm. "Non! Attention! Arrêtez!"

She wants me to think I'm not to do the dishes because lunch was a gift and I have so much other cleaning to do. But *I* know: she doesn't want her things anywhere near that kitchen, let alone in the house. She's probably going home to disinfect everything, assuming she still has any disinfectant in her house. That's what I want to think. It's the English lady's kitchen she's avoiding, not the American man's washing. She gathers all her things, puts them back in her basket, and leaves, once again exchanging four kisses with Kathryn and looking at me askance.

We spend the rest of the day in the kitchen: cleaning the walls, ceiling, the floor, and the cabinets, and rewashing and drying all of the laundry that's in the washer and dryer. Neither of us mentions the stove.

By seven o'clock we've finished one room. We have a beachhead. I'm ready to shower, even a forty-five-second shower. Anywhere else, I'd clean the shower while I wash. Not here. Not a chance. In our cache of supplies, I find the special French product for shower cleaning. Kathryn finds the one for the sink. We spend the next thirty minutes trying to scrub and sterilize them. "That's it," I say. "I quit. It's clean enough for this filthy body for forty-five seconds."

I step into the shower and soap myself in hot water and rinse and shampoo in cold. I finally understand why the French have a bazillion hair products. It's not hair texture, color, length, or health that matters but the temperature of the water in which the hair is being washed: arctic cold, winter cold, cold cold, luke cold, or plain cold. I get dressed while Kathryn waits for the water to reheat so she can shower. Then she gets dressed and we head out to eat.

"Let's picnic," she says.

It's 8:00 in the evening and bright as day. I can't imagine we'll find a place to buy food, but I follow Kathryn's directions as she navigates toward the ocean. In Plomodiern, I see a man locking the door of a *charcuterie*. I pull over and stop. Kathryn jumps out, runs to the man, and says something. He shakes his head, No. She says something else and he opens the door. Twenty minutes later she comes out beaming, carrying a plastic sack, a baguette, and a bottle of wine.

"What did you say to him?"

"I told him we've been working all day and lost track of the time and we're hungry."

"*That* did it?"

"No. I told him we just arrived from America. 'Ah,' he said, 'I thought you were English. Come in.'"

"Where now?"

"The beach. Sainte Anne la Palud."

I've been in France less than twenty-four hours, long enough to know not to have great expectations. We *could* be heading toward a beautiful, natural, protected beach, like the beaches I spent my summers on as a kid—Brighton, Rockaway, Jones Beach, and Fire Island, with velvety white sand and clean, warmish, *swimmable* water. We could *also* be heading toward a rock-strewn, man-made inlet filled with garbage, seaweed, and jellyfish, with scrotum-crunching cold water like the northern Pacific and forty thousand campers, each with three kids, a TV, stereo, grill, and two dogs packed closer together than ants in a hill.

I follow the signs to *la plage* and park in a designated parking place, the only person in the lot to do so, maybe the only person in France. I get out of the car and climb the dunes, expecting anything but what I see. The tide is out, and it's at least one thousand yards of glittery white sand—ten football fields—to the sea. The beach is a natural cove sandwiched between two heather-covered cliffs. The ocean is the color of jade.

We unfold the blanket, sit in the dunes, and eat a chewy white bread called *le zig-zag*, pâté de campagne, two cheeses, Morbier and a Pont l'Éveque that smells to me like rot. We also have a bottle of Vouvray and a salade niçoise and for dessert a mini tarte tatin. It's every bit as good as it sounds, even the Pont l'Éveque. When we finish, I walk to the sea. Fifteen hundred yards—the beach is *fifteen* football fields long. I put my foot in the water. It's warm and pristine, with groups of little fishies still in school swimming around my toes. The foam is like a scallop of lace. On the drive back we stop at a *glacier* on a larger, also beautiful beach in another natural cove between two heather-covered cliffs, and have ice cream on the terrace, under the moon, listening to the incoming surf.

It takes four more days to clean the house, during which we establish a routine. I get up first, dress, and jump out the window. I never do get the lock. I go to the *boulangerie* and buy the same thing: a baguette and two croissants. The second day I come in a look of panic crosses the baker's face—as in, Jesus, what will he want today? In the U.S., the guy would have been overjoyed to see me. Like, holy cow, I'm really going to get my money from yesterday. Not this guy. He's terror-stricken. I can see it in his eyes. All he wants is to do his job, get it right, make someone happy, and here I am screwing him up, *again*. No one else tests his mettle. Everyone else knows what they want, how to ask for it, and how to pay. What he can't see is I'm more terrified than he is. The issue for both of us is, Who's the idiot? In the U.S., I'd try to make it him. Here, there's no question: it's me. It's always me. Every day—in a zillion ways. What's interesting is how we approach it. Without either one of us acknowledging it, we try to help out the other. I, by buying the same thing every day. He, by giving it to me before I ask, point, or beg. It goes like this.

I enter the shop around 7:00 a.m. and say "Bonjour" as soon as I push then pull the door open. The regulars and the baker all say "Bonjour" right back to me. I then take my place in the wedge and add my voice to the "Bonjours" whenever a new person arrives. When it's my turn—it's still unbelievable to me how long it takes each person to tell the baker how she is, make up her mind about what to buy, and pay—the baker treats me like a regular. He says, "Ça va?" I say, "Bon," and ask, "Et vous?" He says, "Ça va." That's it. Meanwhile, he's bagged my croissants, and in acknowledgment of my foreignness and my assumed—no matter how filthy I'm dressed—concern with sanitariness, he wraps a piece of paper around my still warm baguette. Nobody else gets the paper. They take it hand to hand. To pay, I reach in my pocket and hold out a handful of coins for him to take what he wants. Then I say, "Merci. Au revoir," and he says, "Merci. Bonne journée."

I bring the goodies back to Chez Sally, always stopping and saying "Merci" and "Bonjour" to the World War I infantryman. Then we eat and clean. Madame arrives a little before noon to survey our progress, make sure I'm doing my part, and feed us. She brings us lettuce, onions, green beans, potatoes, shallots, radishes, carrots, and leeks from her garden, sometimes still warm from the earth. She also brings eggs from Monsieur Charles and melt-in-your-mouth, soothing-to-eat crêpes wrapped in tinfoil and covered in cloth to stay warm.

On the third day she asks Kathryn where we buy our bread. Kathryn tells her and Madame says "Bon," it's good bread, the best, "meilleur," because the baker is a "spécialiste, un artisan." She's even more impressed when Kathryn tells her *I* buy the bread and decided which *boulangerie* to go to. I don't bother telling her about my first morning and the lady with the dog and the direction her baguette pointed. I can see I'm looking better in Madame's eyes, and that's a good place to be.

After lunch, we clean until 7:30 or 8:00, take our forty-five-second hot showers, and drive back to the same charcuterie, where Kathryn buys different wine (Muscadet, Champigny,

Anjou); cheese (Cantal, bleu d'Auvergne, Livarot); pâté (goose, chicken, pork); and ham (Bayonne, Vendée, jambon de Paris, salami). I had no idea you could do so many things with a pig. Then we drive to a different beach—Bénodet, Morgat, Tréboul, Pointe du Toulinguet, Cap Coz—and picnic. The sea changes color every day—opalescent, mother-of-pearl, diamond, lapis lazuli, emerald, turquoise—depending on the sky, time, clouds, weather, and light. It's the reason Gaugin lived in Pont-Aven and Monet, Signac, and Seurat came to Brittany. The only marring sites are the concrete and rebar German bunkers that string the coast like prehistoric markers, a reminder that nowhere is safe, nothing is perfect, and even in beauty, evil can exist.

At the end of the week, the house is clean and we're ready to write. I carry my computer and books to the third floor, the *deuxième étage*, and find Kathryn's already there. "Hey," I call, "what's this?"

"What?"

"How come you get the third floor? I want the third floor. I get up first and want to be able to work."

"You can work on the second floor. I can't stand the sound of the traffic."

"You live in New York, for Christ's sake. I live in California, in the hills, near a park, where it's quiet. You're used to the noise. I'm not."

"*That's* why! *You* have quiet all the time. You should be more considerate."

This from the person who took the space without asking. If she were French, the baker, for example, I would have made this a win-win. But she's American, and so am I, and I'll be damned if I'm going to lose. "Let's flip a coin," I say, and call heads before she can object. I lose. "Okay. Fair's fair, but *you* clean the stove."

She looks at me as if I'm crazy. "What are you talking about? One thing has nothing to do with another. Let's flip." She takes the coin from my hand and calls tails. I lose again.

It's one of the filthiest, nastiest jobs I've ever done, ranking right down there with cleaning latrines at Boy Scout camp. It takes me half a day. I'm absolutely black, covered with I cannot even imagine what on my face, arms, hair. I stink from the oven, sweat, and special cleaning products for stoves, ovens, and grease. Madame comes in and sees me. I expect the worst, looking the way I do. But she smiles, outright beams, lets out that long, multioctave "Aaaaaah," and gives me four kisses, two on each cheek. That's it. From that moment on, Madame thinks I'm okay.

She walks through the house, room by room, looking and approving, giving it the Madame Seal of Approval and becoming outright joyous. Why not? This is the French at their best: being helpful, of real assistance in a crisis, making a difference, being friendly, genial—*gentil*—Lafayette saving America, Jacques Cousteau saving the sea, Docteurs Sans Borders saving the world, being clean and *propre*—and blaming the whole *catastrophe* on the English. To be able to help and clean and blame the English all in the same act, it's a French dream come true.

Kathryn and I thank her profusely for everything and invite her and Monsieur to dinner the following week. They accept, then we accept their invitation, and they accept ours again and again, all summer.

Monsieur is retired from the navy and rarely leaves the house, but he drives us three hours north to show us Île-de-

Bréhat. Madame hates to leave the earth and hates open water and boats even more, and she braves the fifteen-minute ferry ride to Bréhat. Philippe, their elder son, career navy, solid as a house, several times national black-belt karate champion, fluent in English, lover of the Doors, visits from Cherbourg with his wife and two children, and introduces me to chouchen (fermented honey), lambig (Breton whiskey), and Adelscott (beer laced with whiskey). I reciprocate by sharing two of the three bottles of Macallan's I brought and give him the third when he leaves. Henri, their younger son, who is also fluent in English, is living in Brest, studying to be an emergency medical technician. He and his girlfriend, Renée, return for Sunday family meals, to which Kathryn and I are invited as if we're family. Three or four nights a week and at least one day a weekend we spend with Monsieur and Madame and their family. Monsieur and Madame don't speak English, and I don't speak French, and none of it seems to matter. Mostly what we do is laugh, and not all the time about me.

One night, there's a knock on the door. In the U.S., I'd assume a salesperson, Jehovah's Witnesses, or the FBI. In France, I assume it's Madame P or someone from her family. I open the door, and to my surprise a very pretty woman, with long, dark hair and smelling like a flower, is standing there holding a book with an English title. She's not dressed like any Frenchwoman I've seen, more like a clean grown-up hippie in an ankle-length, colorful Indian print skirt. I point to the book and ask, "You speak English?"

"Of course, I'm Canadian. I'm here to return Sally's book."

I invite her in. We discuss books and writing and fiction. She, Sharon, is a serious, critical, and intelligent reader who has read lots of American authors. She invites us for *apéritifs* the following night at her house. *Apéritifs* means drinks. No dinner. The commitment is safe and proscribed: drink, nibble, talk, go home. It's for a few hours, not a lifetime.

Kathryn and I arrive on time, 7:30, the time Sharon told us, which is the wrong time, because in France only the trains and planes are on time, and she isn't ready. I offer to help, but she doesn't let me. Nobody lets me. Madame P won't even let me clear the table or go anywhere near her kitchen.

We sit in the living room, and their two boys—Yann, about fourteen, and Noé, about ten—come out of their rooms to entertain us. Come *out* of their rooms! They shake my hand, kiss Kathryn on the cheek, and sit down. Her husband, Jean, enters, does the same, and says, "Hello." He looks like the French intellectuals I see in movies: tan and thin, with longish, over-the-collar, over-the-forehead, prematurely graying hair that somehow looks both distinguished and casual, glasses hanging from a string around his neck, wearing non-pressed jeans and a loose, baggy sweater. He has the demeanor of gravitas and the voice of reason—as if he could explain anything. If he weren't curious and didn't have an easy laugh and the twinkle of amusement in his eyes, he'd be intimidating. But he's engaging and, as with Sharon, I like him immediately.

Sharon finally joins us, and we sit for a couple of hours drinking kir, whiskey, and Ricard, finishing a bag of peanuts, two dry sausages, several tomatoes, chips, olives, radishes from their garden, and cornichons. By 9:30, I'm sloshed, and the boys, who sit through the whole thing, must be starving. Jean invites us to dinner, and the conversation changes from the political and social—basically what's wrong with the U.S.—to the personal. We tell them who we are, why we're here, and what we're doing. Sharon tells us she's Irish and

Jean's Breton and they met in Montreal in the sixties where he worked as a filmmaker. Jean tells us about the feature film he's made about television being introduced into a tiny, rural village in India and that he's currently writing a book about consciousness, melding Eastern religion and philosophy with Western philosophy and science. Sharon works with physically and developmentally disabled adults and is an abstract painter. We leave at two-thirty in the morning—the boys go to sleep at about one—and invite them all to dinner at Chez Sally the following week.

I have lived in the Oakland hills fifteen years and don't know any of my neighbors. I have lived in France less than a month and know two families, one of which doesn't speak English, and have a social life more full and active than I do in the States. All my life, I've disdained the connectedness, closeness, visibility, complicity—the busybodiness and dependence of small-town and suburban life, and here, in Brittany, in this village of five hundred people, I find I desire it: the coziness of it, the togetherness, the *neighborliness*, knowing there's a place where, whoever you are, you are known. I don't know why I feel this, but I do, and I know I'm going to miss this life and these people when I leave.

Market Day

Thursday is market day in Loscoat, and I'm going shopping with Madame P. I know this because she's standing in the doorway of Chez Sally with her car in front of the house, the passenger door open and the engine running. I'm trying to explain that it's raining, when I realize (1) she already knows, and (2) it doesn't matter. Bretons sprout umbrellas the way Texans sprout guns. Umbrella in one hand, panier in the other, they're ready to shop. That I have no interest or desire or need to see a bunch of farmers selling fruit and veggies in the rain doesn't matter any more than any of the other things I had no desire to see or do that I've done. Madame wants me to go to the market, so I'm going.

I sit in the car and watch as she S-turns, barely missing the edge of the quay and toppling us into the river, and gets to

Loscoat faster than until that moment I would have believed humanly possible. She parks on the sidewalk and decars, snaps open her umbrella—a basic black that covers the two of us—puts her purse in the panier, and we head out, armed. Using the cane basket as a lance and battering ram, sharp eyes, and lots of distracting questions, we go from stall to stall. "What's this?" "Where does that come from?" "What's in it?" "How old?" "How much?" With each question she samples the wares, an apricot here, cherries there, honey cake, cheese, sausage. Clearly, I'm in the presence of a pro. She buys with the eyes of a diamond broker looking for flaws.

She hands me a peach. I roll it over in my palm and give it back to her. "Bonne," I say. "Bien. Joli." She gives me an avocado and indicates I should squeeze it. I do. I also smell a melon on the same spot she does, and bite into a strawberry from Plougastel that's so sweet it makes the first bite into a stick of Juicy Fruit taste like alum. Everything's "bonne, bien, and joli." I stay with her until the rain lightens up, then wander off.

I expected the market to be tiny and dull, and it's neither. It's on both sides of the river, and the array of goods for sale is astounding: beds, mattresses, furniture, insurance, vacuum cleaners, driver's education classes, bric-a-brac, and the strangest selection of women's undergarments I've ever seen—a cross between the Marquis de Sade and Grandma Rose: girdles the size and strength of truck gaskets, bras with so much metal in them they could be soup tureens, panties like hot-air balloons. Africans are selling goods made in Africa and China. There are pizzas to go, paella and Vietnamese food, lots of flower sellers, people who specialize in spices, cheese, meats, kitchen supplies and utensils, fish, pocketbooks, historical postcards, wine, and tablecloths. Three guys stand in front of a stainless-steel van that in the U.S. would be an Airstream camper and in France is a giant rotisserie with a dozen chickens and a two-hundred-pound pig rotating on spits as if they're on a Florida beach trying to get an even tan. The pig still has his head and feet. His brother's on the counter, half gone. I buy a slice of him for lunch and search for a chicken to cook for dinner.

I don't want one of the rotating chickens because Europe's largest chicken-processing company, Doux, is in the next village, and I've heard and smelled what they do to their birds. I want a free-range chicken, not one of their concentration-camp types, which is what I suspect the rotisserie guys use because they're cheapest. The problem is how to find one—and how to say it. My first thought is *libre* (which actually is correct, as in *liberty*) but dismiss it because I think it also means free of charge, and I don't want to be asking some French person for a free chicken.

I walk about practicing what I'm going to say, looking for someone who is alone, so no one else will hear me, someone who looks simpatico, so I won't be a bigger fool than I am. I walk past a couple of *charcuterie* stands with wedges of people and several butchers who look forbidding. Toward the end of the quay I spot a slight man with a big smile standing alone in front of a van the size of an ice cream truck with Poulet Fermier written on the side. It's an omen, a sign from the shopping god. I rush to him before anyone else arrives—he must think I'm desperate for a chicken—and say in my most polished, assured voice, "Monsieur, avez vous une poulet au beaucoup de promenade?"

He doesn't even flinch. "Oui," he says, and opens the back of his van and removes three birds. "Noir, blanc, ou rouge?"

"Qu'est-ce que c'est, le difference?"

It's the right thing to say, because Monsieur has an unbelievable amount to tell me about these birds. Unfortunately, I don't understand any of it, but I do my part by interjecting an occasional "oui," "ah," and a "bonne." Ten minutes later, having either finished or given up, he picks up *le rouge*, turns it over, spreads its legs, and puts it down. He does the same with *le blanc* and *le noir*. I'm looking between the legs of these chickens for I don't know what, hoping Madame doesn't walk past and catch me. "Bonne," I say. "Bien. C'est joli."

He hands me the black. "C'est le meilleur."

I hold out my money and watch as he carefully counts seventy-five francs (about fifteen dollars), and writes 75 on a piece of paper and hands it to me along with a plastic bag of innards, neck, feet, and for all I know, the head. Who knows what the French won't eat? I walk toward the car with a chicken in one plastic bag and a slice of pig in another, feeling as if I'd survived a potentially life-threatening incident, when I see a man in blue overalls gently lifting the side-panel door of his van. The van is higher and longer than all the others, and he's raising the panel as if the van contains Fabergé eggs. I stop, and watch, and listen to what sounds like birds—and see it is. Hundreds of them in cages: finches, budgies, canaries, parakeets, cockatiels, parrots, a macaw, a toucan—squeaking, squawking, shrieking, chirping, looking stunned and bewildered by their ride, like where am I and how did I get here? I've never seen or heard anything like it. A dozen villagers and I stand there amused and transfixed and surprised, everyone smiling as if we've just seen a rainbow or been to the circus or heard a Mozart concerto.

The following week I go to the market alone. I've managed to purchase fresh pasta from the butter, egg, and cheese lady by pointing to it, holding up two fingers and saying, "Pour deux." Emboldened, I search for a bay leaf for the sauce. I know what bay leaves look like and how they smell, so I approach the spice, herb, and condiment lady with confidence.

"Bonjour," I say.

"Bonjour," she says, and we're off.

I walk to the left, the right, back and forth several times. I see cumin, curry, paprika, cinnamon, nutmeg, tarragon; white, red, and black pepper; coconut, mustard, cardamom, oregano, marjoram, rosemary, parsley, sage, thyme, pickles, roasted peppers, olives, eggplant—everything except bay leaves. Can this be? Do bay leaves look different here? I walk away and return, certain I'm missing it, which is often the case in France. On my third return the lady says, "Monsieur?"— always the beginning of trouble.

I know what I want, but I don't know how to say it. I was so sure I'd find it, I didn't bother looking up the word. I try, "Avez vous le bay leaf?"

She looks blank.

"Bay-leaf."

She looks puzzled. I can see she's starting to panic.

"*Bay* leaf." For some reason I've convinced myself it's the same word in French, and all I have to do is find the right accent. I lower my voice and say, "Bay *leaf.*"

"*Moment,*" she says, and does something I've never seen any seller at the market do. She leaves her stall and goes to the fellow in the stall next to her, a guy selling hats, and says something to him, pointing at me, and says in a lowered voice, "Bay *leaf.*"

He says, "Quoi?"

"*Bay* leaf," she repeats.

"*Bay* leaf?"

50

Now they're both muttering it and looking at me. "Qu'est-ce que c'est *bay* leaf?"

The lady returns shaking her head, obviously dismayed at the loss of the sale, not knowing what I mean, maybe failing France, who knows?

"Merci," I say, and walk away, not wanting to cause her any more consternation.

A few minutes later I return. The spice lady is smiling. She's talking to a customer she can actually help. When she sees me she smiles wider, but in my heart I know it's a wince. I'm convinced, though, I can convey what I want and save us both. The satisfied customer leaves happy with a plastic bag filled with five olives. I wait for her to get out of hearing and sight, then walk up to the spice lady and say, "Madame."

"Oui . . .?" She makes it a question.

I remove the pasta from my shopping bag. She looks at me as if I pulled a rabbit out of a hat. "Le pâtes," I say, and hold it up to indicate I'm not talking about pastry *le pâte*.

"Oui . . . ?"

"Le espice pour la sauce de pâtes."

She stares at me, speechless. Luckily this is Brittany. She's too polite to hate me.

"Madame," I say, trying to get her attention back, as I see her eyes are glazed and she's fading. "Le sauce tomate pour le pâtes, oui . . ."

"Oui."

"C'est necessaire le espice specialment pour la sauce."

She says nothing.

"*Bay* leaf," I say. "Bay *leaf.*"

She holds up thyme, marjoram, rosemary, coriander, paprika—who knows what foreigners eat with pasta?—anything she can think of, trying to help or get rid of me.

"Merci," I say, and walk away defeated, leaving her and the hat guy muttering, "*Bay leaf.*" I'm so rattled I buy a bag of honey soap from the honey lady and leave it at the stall.

On my way to the car, the chicken guy sees me and calls, "Monsieur."

Shit. Now he thinks I'm a regular and I'm going to get the hard sell.

"Oui . . .?" I say. I say it the way the spice lady said it to me.

"Comment est le poulet au beaucoup d'promenade?" he says and smiles, and I know he's been telling this story all week.

"Bien. Bonne. C'est joli."

He smiles wider. I'm happy too. At least one French person understands me.

I return to Chez Sally and look bay leaf up in the dictionary. *Laurier.* Laurel. No wonder the spice lady and hat guy couldn't get it.

Madame P knocks on the door. I brew tea and explain in great detail about "bay leaf" and *laurier*. She laughs and laughs and laughs, harder than usual, I think, then takes me by the hand and leads me outside. "Laurier," she says, pulling a leaf from a tree and putting it under my nose. No wonder the spice lady doesn't sell bay leaves. They grow wild, *everywhere*. No French person in her right mind would pay for something she can get for free.

The next Thursday I go to the market, hoping to avoid the spice lady, feeling like a total jerk. I see a wedge of people in front of her stall, people buying three or four olives at a time, and scurry past.

"Monsieur."

Shit.

I walk over, prepared to be humiliated. "Madame."

She reaches under the counter and holds up a three-foot branch covered with bay leaves. "Laurier," I say, at the same time she and the hat guy say, "Bay *leaf.*" I can't believe she brought an entire branch of it to the market for me.

I thank her and walk through the market proudly carrying my branch like the laurel it is. Someone taps me on the shoulder. I turn around. It's the honey lady. "Monsieur," she says, and hands me the bars of soap I bought and left at her stall last week. She's held them all week, like the spice lady, not knowing if or when I'd return. Now she'll never get rid of me. I'll never buy honey or honey products from anyone else. Or spices. Or cheese. Or pasta. For as long as I'm here, I'm hooked.

Pardon Moi

The second Sunday in July is the *Pardon* of Locronan. Madame P tells me I should go. I wonder if it's like Nixon and Watergate, and who's being pardoned for what? I read the guidebook to see what I'm getting into and see it's not politics or crime but religion. Of course! This is Catholic-land with a Gothic *C*. Every village has a saint, and every saint has its day, and every *day* has its saint. Clearly, these are not a people who want to take their chances with God. Madame P wears multiple charms—Saint Anne, Mary, and Saint Rita—and has reliquaries from Lourdes and Rome in her dining room and a crucifix on the wall next to the front door for protection in this world and insurance in the next.

As a kid growing up in Brooklyn and Long Island, I was jealous and disdainful of my Catholic friends who went to priests and made confessions any day or time of the week and were absolved for anything bad they'd said or thought or done. In those days, church doors were always open. Today the church has discovered the market economy (not to mention the joys of litigation) and has economized—fewer priests, fewer masses, fewer confessions, and fewer churches open fewer hours—so Pardon day is the day to do it. Makes sense to me, a one-stop, one-shop kind of day. What doesn't make sense is why Madame wants *me* to go. I don't know if it's to see a tourist attraction, like Île Bréhat, or because I'm a desecrater of all things revered in France, like language, attire, and protocol. Does it mean she thinks there's hope for me, or I'm already lost? What? What?

The Pardon starts at two-thirty, after lunch, because everything important in France starts after lunch, and the people leading the procession will need all the strength they can get. I arrive at two o'clock because I'm American enough to believe things start on time, and earlier is better than later. I park the car and walk into the village carrying the brochure the Lady of the Parking Lot gave me.

The closer I get to *centre-ville* the more improbable the village becomes. It looks like a perfectly reconstructed medieval village, right down to the few old people in traditional costumes strategically placed at conspicuous locations—a Breton Williamsburg or Old Sturbridge Village. Only this is real.

The church is fifteenth-century, Gothic. The houses are sixteenth- and seventeenth-century Renaissance, and everything—*everything*—is built with granite: the church, houses, cobbled streets, dormers, stairs, ramps, shops, benches, tombstones. Geraniums are everywhere, in pots, planters, growing from the ground, turning the village into a cross between a nursery and graveyard. The windows of the houses are curtained with lace, each house with its own design: tiny boats in the sea, fishermen, boys and girls playing on the beach, flowers, gardens, Breton people in medieval costumes. It's as if there were a village competition and the whole village won. Except for the people on the street, it's a still life, a memento mori, all of it watched over by midget, carved-in-granite, local, Breton saints. They're perched in niches built above doors or windows, below the roofs, into the sides of the houses, or set on lawns, waiting, watching, blessing, judging every human thing that happens. The whole scene is so perfect it could be Hollywood. The brochure tells me it *is* Hollywood. More than thirty films have been shot here, including Roman Polanski's *Tess of the d'Urbervilles*. For all I know, this village is Brittany's Schwab's.

I round the bend and see hundreds of tourists with cameras, guidebooks, water bottles, and backpacks, milling in front of the church. It's like the annual Macy's sale is about to begin, or trying to get tickets to the Rolling Stones. The French are in restaurants and on the terraces, in the parking lots and picnic areas, eking out every millisecond of eating they can. Watching them makes me hungry.

I get in a line for crêpes to go. Brits, Germans, and Americans are ahead of me, people who excel at lining up, so the line moves quickly. "Beurre et sucre," I say to myself, rehearsing as I wait my turn, "Beurre et sucre," and search my pockets for the correct change. The girl behind the counter may look a kindly fifteen, but to me she's Marie Antoinette.

"Beurre et sucre," I say when I reach the counter.

"Butter and sugar," she repeats, making sure we've both got it right. Then she spreads the thinnest layer of batter possible over a round, sizzling, butter-greased grill, waits a few seconds for the edges to become crispy and tan, flips it over, drops two more tablespoons of butter on it, sprinkles sugar, folds it in half, melts more butter, more sugar, folds it in fourths, and wraps it in wax paper and hands it to me. "Beurre et sucre," she says.

No kidding. I give her the money, step aside, bite into it, and burn the roof of my mouth. Butter drips over my hand and down my arm. I gobble it as fast as I can, then lick my fingers, hand, and arm like a cat cleaning his paws. There's no way to eat this without making a mess, and they don't give you a napkin. For a people crazed by cleanliness . . . I *get* it! This isn't about *my* cleanliness, or even France's—that's my business and France's. This is about the crêpe lady's expenses. Napkins cost money, and she'll be damned if she's going to pay her money to keep me (and France) clean. It's Milton Friedman market-based economy to the core, and the reason I can't get ice cubes, decent toilet paper, towels, soap, or shampoo in hotels. If I want those conveniences, I should bring them. I wipe my hands on my pants and wait.

At three o'clock, the church doors open. It's a good thing, because half the crowd is ready to faint. The sun ricocheting off the granite is causing sunspots and increasing the already hot temperature several degrees. A gray-haired priest in a for-est-green robe steps through the doors carrying a huge silver staff with a gold Jesus stretched on the cross.

The priest is surrounded by young boys in white, swing-ing censers. He says something in Breton, another language I don't understand, then walks down the stairs and enters the crowd, which has grown to thousands, as the French have quit eating and joined the group.

Following the priest are more young boys in white, other

priests, acolytes, and guys in suits, probably the mayor and other politicos, and following them are the villagers. It looks like a Happening, Sergeant Pepper reprised: men with Abe Lincoln beards and sideburns to rival Elvis's, wearing Amish-like hats and brightly embroidered vests with jackets and waistcoats embroidered to match, wide breeches and striped pantaloons, and thick leather belts or colorful sashes as cummerbunds; women wearing lace hats of varying heights, widths, curls, flips, flaps, twists, bends, and stitches to indicate what village they're from. (It's the semiotics of the Middle Ages. No wonder Derrida is French.) Blouses are embroidered in phosphorescent orange, black, white, reds, and blues, often all on the same person, with a complementing skirt, jacket, and an apronlike piece of cloth over everything—and *everything* is edged with lace. The children are wearing miniature versions of the same.

Hundreds of people exit the church and march around the square, which is so crowded it's a miracle anyone can move, especially now, with the people emerging from the church carrying heavy, hulky, bulky, unbalanced, barely manageable, large and small pieces of church reliquary and dozens of colorful banners for Saint Ronan (the patron saint of Locronan), Mary, Anne, Margaret, as well as the bier of Saint Ronan; a giant cross; everything, it seems, except the altar, pews, and organ. It's ingenious. I've got to hand it to those Catholics. What better test of faith, belief, rectitude, and submission than to march around town carrying hernia-inducing reliquary in ninety-degree heat, wearing dark, heavy clothes in July?

The priest begins to sing. Everyone in the procession joins him. They seem to be marching in groups—Our Ladies for Mary, Men for Saint Joseph, Our Ladies of Good News—

but I can't tell. The procession is huge and long, hundreds of people, with thousands of others lining the way, watching as they pass by. It's the first time I've seen French people form a straight line. They march. They stop. They sing. They march. The rear can't see the front. The front can't see the rear. They're following the path of Saint Ronan, an Irish hermit who lived and preached in Locronan in the fifth century. Lucky for the kids and the people carrying the reliquary, this is a Petite Troménie, only three or four kilometers (about two miles) to the chapel on top of the hill, not the Grande Troménie, which happens once every six years and requires circling the entire village, walking through the surrounding woods and up the hill for twelve kilometers. It happens once every six years because it takes five years to recuperate. To prove the point, an old guy, one of six carrying a larger-than-life-size wooden saint, mutters to his buddy, "C'est plus mauvais que la guerre." It's worse than the war.

Two hours into the march people are sweating and breathing hard. Many have produced bottles of water from somewhere in their garb, but as far as I can see nobody has quit or dropped out. Amazing as that is, two other things amaze me more. One, there are no police. I mention this later to Sharon and Jean, and they shake their heads in dismay. "They're there," Sharon says. "*You* don't see them," Jean adds. I don't know if they're right or paranoid or both, or if French police have the best PR in the world: French people think they're everywhere, so in reality they don't have to be anywhere. It's a mystery I've yet to solve. All I know is, if an entire village were on the march in the U.S., the police would make a point of being visible. But that observation is nothing compared to the second one: teenagers are here. Willingly, smilingly walking with their family, holding hands with siblings *and* parents, not sulking or being dragged by the hair. I haven't seen anything like it since *Father Knows Best* went off the air.

It takes three hours to reach the chapel. Given the heat and the clothes and the stopping, singing, praying, marching, and handing off of reliquary from carrier to carrier like a relay, it's not bad.

I bring up the rear, as I seem to do a lot here. I turn the final bend and see the chapel—the chapel *I* thought was the goal, the purpose, our destiny. I must be the only one who thought so, because not a single person is there, including the priests and the suits. They are wedged up to a makeshift bar drinking beer, hard cider, and Breton whiskey. Other people stand in front of the stage waiting for the band—drums, oboe, bagpipe, and accordion. Boys and girls play peacefully with each other. There's no pushing, shoving, teasing, or taunting. The teenagers are smoking, the men and women drinking beer, all in full costume, nobody rushing home to change clothes or watch TV. The band starts to play and people hold hands and form circles, and circles within circles within circles, and everyone begins bouncing up and down like yo-yos, which I guess to them is dancing. It's part religion, part tradition, part myth, and part civic duty—and all the parts seem to fit together, at least for today.

It reminds me of July Fourth and the small town I grew up in in the 1950s, and I wonder what in the world would get me to join and enjoy something so hokey in the U.S. today? I look for fissures, breaks, anything disruptive, disjointive, forced, out of place, and for the life of me I can't see it. For the moment *I* even feel as if I fit in. I came to Locronan prepared to mock the seriousness of what couldn't be serious and the hypocrisy of acting like it is. I leave with the joy of seeing and being part of this communal experience. Either I'm fooling myself, or Brittany is fooling me. Either way, it works.

I don't know if I've been pardoned or not; I didn't pray or sing. But Madame P is happy I went, and that's enough for me. She rewards me with a smile, the double-cheek kiss, and a pudding dessert. *Far Breton*, she calls it. I call it far out. Who would have guessed you could make anything that good with prunes? Talk about a miracle!

Fête Nautique

On my way to buy bread one morning I see a sign in Place Charles de Gaulle: *Fête Nautique*. Nautical fete. I know what that means: boats. Beneath, it says *feu d'artifice*.

I ask Monsieur P, "Qu'est-ce que c'est, feu d'artifice?"

He looks up in the sky, raises his arms straight over his head, and brings them down on either side of him in a woosh, saying, "Booom."

I think he's telling me again about the munitions factory in a nearby town that blew up during the revolution. What that has to do with *fête nautique* I don't know, but I also don't know how to ask.

That was on a Monday.

On the Friday of the weekend of the fête I drive into Loscoat and see a camel tied to the fence along the quay. No one but me seems to find this interesting or odd, which is interesting in itself, because in my brief experience here, people are curious about everything. Everything except this camel, which probably means it's not new, unexpected, or a surprise, though it's the first time *I've* seen a camel in town.

I drive back to Plobien to tell Monsieur P and get stuck in a traffic jam of Mercedes vans and trailers. I follow them as far as Chez Sally and watch as they stop, pull over, and park in front of the church and *mairie*.

Monsieur P is sitting in a chair in his driveway, sunbathing. I tell him about the camel, or try to, then give up. Instead, I point to the vans and trailers and say, "Qu'est-ce que c'est?"

"Pour la fête."

"Ah. Oui." I haven't a clue.

That evening, after dinner, I take my usual stroll along the river road to the viaduct, but I don't make it past the village square. Place Charles de Gaulle has been turned into a small-town suburban carnival. In front of the church and *mairie* are a tiny Ferris wheel and merry-go-round for little kids, bumper cars for bigger kids, and at least a dozen sideshows for everyone—shoot the duck, catch the fish, hook the cow, hoop the pig, eat the sausage, nuts, nougat, cotton candy, pastry, and have a beer—and the whole *place* is practically empty. It's as if they're having a party and no one comes. It's sad, actually, so I buy a stick of blue cotton candy and shoot some ducks to make the concessionaires happy and give them hope.

Saturday is also quiet. Activity picks up a little at night with a few teens, but basically it's dead. I have no idea how these people stay in business. It's one of the sorriest sights I've seen: a sad, empty, lonely fair, enough to make a Toulouse-Lautrec look cheerful.

Sunday is more of the same. Actually, it's a little worse because not even the teens are there. They prefer the bench at the bus stop to the fair. *No one* is interested. *I'm* getting depressed. Monday is fête night and this little town—*my* little town (I tend to take things personally)—is going to throw a party and no one is going to come. These poor people. How do they afford those Mercedes? It's another example of French capitalism that makes no sense to me.

Monday morning I see men on the other side of the river, a first. All I've seen so far are cows and horses. They walk around the ruins of what I thought was a château and find out later was a prison built by Napoleon, banging things into the ground and leaving tiny black boxes behind them. It looks like some kind of secret commando operation. Maybe it is a secret commando operation, and daylight is their cover. This is what happens when I don't know what's going on: I become paranoid.

In the afternoon, I'm startled out of sleepy oblivion by Mick Jagger screaming, "I can't get no satisfaction." It's at a brain-piercing decibel level. All afternoon, without warning or discernible pattern, Mick blasts his way through town, drowning out traffic, church bells, and thought, breaking through doors, windows, and three-foot-thick stone walls.

At seven o'clock I go outside to look around. A few people are straggling about, but no more than usual. Basically, the village is empty. The concessionaires are eating their own wares. I don't know if that's good or not—it's so good they're eating it, or no one else is going to eat it, so they might as well. On my way back to Chez Sally I watch three guys open a couple of tables and barricade the road. Either the revolution has come and it's beginning in Plobien or they're going to charge to get into town. Neither one makes any sense. Who's going to pay? Who's even going to be here? It's frustrating understanding so little.

Kathryn and I walk next door to Monsieur and Madame P's, where we're invited for dinner. I expect a full house, the whole family, because the family is the basic social unit in France, not me, me, me, which is difficult for an American to understand, until it's *not* about me and then it's easy.

Philippe, Estelle, their young boy and girl, Deniel and Annick, Henri, and his girlfriend, Renée, are there. So are Monsieur Jacques, an elf of a man with a leprechaun smile, the owner of a huge construction company; Monsieur Robert, a man with arms like oxygen tanks, who, according to Henri, makes the best lambig (whiskey) and venison pâté in Finistère; and Monsieur Charles, the egg man, who lives with forty hens, two roasters, four pigs, a goat, and a dog. I sit between Philippe and Henri. It's my only chance to understand a thing.

The evening starts with sitting in the living room and drinking *apéritifs* for an hour: peach kir, strawberry kir, cherry, blackberry, raspberry kir, kir Breton with cider, kir royale with champagne, and for the more adventurous, Monsieur Robert's lambig, which could strip paint from a table and six chairs in ten minutes. There's juice and water for the kids.

Through the window, I see a few people walking into town. "How many people do you think will be here tonight?" I ask Philippe.

"Three or four thousand."

"Thousand?" I think he's using the old numbers the way everyone else does, even though the "new" numbers have been in effect for twenty years, and he really means 4 or 40 or 400. "The village has only five hundred people."

He shrugs. *"Normal."*

We sit down to dinner at eight o'clock, thirteen of us and the dog. I'm halfway looped. Kathryn is three-quarters. The meal, like most meals, begins with melon. That's what it's called, melon. It looks like cantaloupe but is smaller and sweeter. Madame serves each adult three huge slices, and we're off to another French meal. Melon is followed by crudité, a salad of red lettuce from her garden, eggs from Monsieur Charles, and tomatoes from the market—hers won't be ready until August—with lots of fresh bread and mounds of butter and an endless supply of rosé. After the crudité, she serves generous slices of pink ham garnished with cornichons, mustard, homemade mayonnaise, and more fresh bread and butter and white wine. Thank God, I think, a light meal, and help myself to several moist slices of jambon supérieur. Meanwhile, families are arriving carrying chairs, umbrellas, bottles of water, backpacks, fanny packs, children, and dogs. Two women carry cats. For all I know there are also rabbits, chickens, and baby pigs. When French people aren't eating their animals, they love them.

By 9:30, I'm bursting and ready to go outside. That's when Madame brings the main course—three platters, each the size of a Cadillac hubcap, dripping with browned, already cut-up, covered in their own juices, chickens from Monsieur Charles, two bowls of rice, and potatoes and green beans from her garden, with more butter and bread. Chicken is the sign for Monsieur P to open the red.

By 10:30, we've gone through five bottles of red, two white, two rosé, a few glasses of lambig, several loaves of bread, a half kilo of butter, and most of the chicken, rice, potatoes, and green beans. No one can move. At least, the men can't. Madame, Renée, and Estelle clear the table. Monsieur Jacques groans. The women return with clean plates and silverware, two bowls of butter lettuce from Madame's garden, more bread, and a half dozen different cheeses. Monsieur Jacques groans louder. I don't have the strength to do that. I slump in my chair and look at the kids.

Deniel is six and Annick is four, and they're sitting through the meal like adults. They talk to the adults. They talk *like* adults. Adults talk to them like adults. They're *dressed* like adults. No one speaks baby talk to them, no one yells at them, and absolutely no one spanks, embarrasses, teases, or humiliates them. They are corrected with a look, a touch, a word— *arrête, doucement, non, écoute*—and they do. In the U.S., these kids would be at a separate table, a separate room, maybe even a separate house or village, eating a separate meal. They'd either be watching TV or demanding something they shouldn't have and wouldn't get, except maybe tonight because they can hold their parents hostage in front of their friends. Not French kids. French parents treat their kids like adults, knowing they're children and they'll lapse. American parents treat their kids like babies and get short with them when they don't act grown up. One of the saddest sights I've seen is American parents bringing their two-year-olds to the movies and getting upset when the babies begin to cry. I remember how well behaved the French kids were on the flight to France and the train ride to Brest, and Yann and Noé, Sharon and Jean's *teenage* boys, coming out of their room to greet us, and the teenagers at Locronan, and the cafés and restaurants filled with multigenerational diners. Children of all ages *with* their parents, everywhere, like tonight, fête night, families outside and family inside, even future family with Renée, everyone doing their part—and everyone has one.

Monsieur opens the wine and tastes it, a job he takes so seriously he's already turned down two bottles of his own as too young. Madame prepares the meal, and she, Estelle, and Renée serve it and clear the table. Deniel and Annick try to act like adults, and for the most part succeed. Even the dog is on his best behavior, staying under the table the entire meal.

All roles and behavior are prescribed. Everyone knows his or her place, has one and *wants* one. The only person resisting is me. I was trained to help clean up after dinner. Every girl-friend I've had has insisted—no matter what I do—that I do more. Yet when I stand to help, I'm told to sit down. When I try to stack plates, I'm told to stop. I'm the guest, *l'invité*, and *invités* are not expected to do anything except indulge. That's *my* role. It's all a little bit retro, like fifties TV sit-coms, *Ozzie and Harriet* and *Leave It to Beaver*, with the zaniness of *I Love Lucy* tossed in. Doctors make home visits here, milk comes in bottles, kids listen, and fresh food isn't packaged in cello-phane. It all feels very familiar to me, though, of course, it's not.

By 11:15, we've finished the salad and cheeses. It's still light out, almost dusk, and everyone wants to go to the fête. I fol-low Henri and Philippe outside and am surprised to see the town is jammed. The entire quay and both sides of the street, several thousand people, with more wedged up to pay at the barricade. We make our way through the crowd toward Place Charles de Gaulle, where everything is. The concessions are going full bore: cotton candy, sausages, candies, nuts, beignets, beer, soda. Philippe goes to a shooting gallery, picks up a rifle, and quickly shoots five ducks. He walks away with a bear the size of Annick. He goes to two other shooting galleries and wins a truck for Deniel and a stuffed rabbit for Estelle.

The one activity I'm familiar with—besides games you can't win, like tossing the coins that bounce off the plate, shooting the balls that won't fit through the net, throwing the balls that can't knock over the bottles—is bumper cars. I pay my way and get in a car. The first time I'm hit, my teeth rattle. I'm thankful they're still mine—if they weren't they'd be on the floor. The only time I've felt anything like this was in an actual car accident. Bang—my neck snaps back. Whiplash. The five-year-old girl who hit me, dressed like a young Loretta Young, giggles maniacally at the sound of my howl and rams me again. My back hurts, my stomach aches. If this ride were in the U.S., lawyers and doctors would be handing out cards, doctors to fix you, lawyers to fix them. The only thing I can figure is it's like those horror movies they show in driver's education classes: this is what an accident feels like, though it certainly hasn't had a deleterious effect on the driving I've seen.

I bought tokens for five rides, but one is enough for me. I stand up, half bent in pain, and wobble off to have a beer with Messieurs Charles, Jacques, and Robert. It's the right thing to do socially, but not gastronomically, after the meal, the wine, and the ride. All I want to do is lie down.

As we walk back toward the house, I see people are still paying to come into town. The wedges at the rides and concessions are thinning as people start to wedge up on the quay. Lots of people have chairs and blankets, a few have tables. Some are standing, others kneeling. There are kids on shoulders and hips, dogs on leashes, strollers with kids and dogs, and somewhere a couple of cats. Again, I'm surprised at the number of families, including teenagers, and the lack (or invisibility) of cops. There's no pushing, no yelling, just several thousand people wedging up at 11:30 at night waiting for something to happen. It's a *fête nautique* and people are facing the river, but I don't see a thing.

I ask Henri, "What are we waiting for?"

"The boats."

"What boats?"

"Floats."

"When does it start?"

"When it gets dark."

We go back to the house and sit on the stone wall facing the river: Monsieur and Madame, Henri, Renée, Philippe with Annick on his lap, Estelle with Deniel on hers, Charles, Jacques, Robert, Kathryn, and I, waiting. Finally, all the lights in the village go off, as if the entire village failed to pay its electric bill, and a voice booms out of the dark.

"Bonsoir!"

"It's the mayor," Philippe says. "He's welcoming everyone and telling them the theme."

"What theme?"

"The theme for tonight."

"There's a theme?"

"Yes, sure. There's always a theme." He says it like *How could you not know?*

I look around. No one is in costume, or at least anything I recognize as a costume, unless everyone is pretending to be an American in their Nikes and Adidas and "I heart Florida" T-shirts. There are no banners, bunting, buttons, flags, nothing out of the usual, except five thousand people in a village of five hundred.

All of a sudden there's wild applause. I think it's because the mayor has stopped speaking, but Philippe nudges me and points to a pinpoint of light on the river. The light appears to be moving toward us. In a few minutes it's followed by another pinpoint of light. Something or things are slowly making their way down river, hence a *fête nautique*.

As the light gets closer, I hear the putt-putt of a tiny outboard engine but still can't see a thing. I wait more patiently than I usually wait for anything. When it finally comes into view I'm baffled. There's a pink papier-mâché car perched on a tiny float with three people in suits getting into it, sitting down, tooting the horn, and getting out. The action is repeated nonstop.

"What's that?" I ask Philippe.

"Don't know."

He asks Estelle. She asks Monsieur Robert. He asks Monsieur Charles, who asks Monsieur Jacques. No one knows.

"What's the theme?" I ask.

"The European Community."

Renée says, "It's a scene from a movie."

"What movie?"

She doesn't know, except it's English. The word goes around. That's England. "Angleterre." Everyone accepts it as normal, *c'est normal*, and applauds.

The next float has a washing machine perched on it and two women washing clothes by hand. We go through all twelve countries, and no one can figure out which one it is, but we all applaud as it passes.

The third float is a windmill—Holland. It lists, and zigs and zags from one side of the river to the other until it runs aground on the other side and gets stuck. A fellow in clogs emerges from behind the windmill and slumps beneath the rotating sail, tending his jug of grog. We applaud and encourage him on.

The last float is France: three guys with red, white, and blue balloons attached to their clothing, who are banging into each other and falling down. I think it's an educational display, like an atom exhibit, maybe nuclear power or a cyclotron—touting French education, science, reason, rationality—until I see the bottles in their hands and realize the balloons are grapes, and the guys are wine. They're falling down smashed, laughing and singing, drinking from the bottles and waving them in the air, jiggling their grapes like pom-poms, the merriest guys in the European Community. I cheer as they float past, amazed they can stand at all.

The lights go off again and the mayor begins speaking in that deep, resonant, grave, official French voice, as if he's telling us the village just won the war or lost the war or is going to war. He makes Winston Churchill and Edward R. Murrow sound like Pépe LePew. I'm thinking about where that French voice comes from, how they conjure it—when a deafening cannonlike blast explodes and reverberates off the stone buildings, followed by a shower of gleaming white stars in the sky. *Feu d'artifice!* That's what Monsieur P was telling me! Fireworks! Fireworks and Mozart.

Rockets, flares, twirly things, sparklers, blossoms on top of blossoms on top of blossoms, reds, blues, whites, greens, gold—for twenty-five minutes, people "Oui-ing" and "Bonne-ing," cheering like it's the coup du monde; Mozart, Vivaldi, Dvořák, Ravel amplify and interpret every blast. They are the most incredible, amazing, startling, beautiful, mesmerizing fireworks I've seen and heard. Whatever people paid, it isn't enough. The show is better than any Fourth of July or Memorial Day celebration in New York, Chicago, or San Francisco. This little village of five hundred people is putting on a world-class fête. The finale is the Big Bang beginnings of Earth: Beethoven and huge blinding explosions followed by darkness, then Debussy and lights.

I'm thrilled and exhausted. Kathryn is, too. We're about to say bonsoir to Madame P and her family when Philippe taps me on the shoulder and introduces me to the mayor, Monsieur L' Guillennec. At forty-seven years old, I've never met a mayor. I've been in the village less than a month and the mayor knows me. "Bonsoir, Marc," he bellows, shaking my hand and adding in English, "Just like in New York, yes!"

"Oui," I say, "Meilleur. Merci, merci beaucoup."

That's it for me. I'm done—but Madame P's not. She calls us in for dessert. Kathryn and I look at each other and understand that any excuse would be hopeless. We shuffle back and take our previous seats, all of us, including the dog. Madame, Renée, and Estelle bring forth platters of desserts as if no one has eaten in days: butter cake *(kouign amann)*; a denser butter cake *(gâteau Breton)*; egg-and-butter pudding *(far Breton)*; butter cookies *(galettes)*; two peach tarts; warm crêpes with butter, strawberry, vanilla, and chocolate ice creams; orange sorbet; several jams; coffee; several teas; and more of Monsieur Robert's all-purpose lambig, which after dinner is called a *digestif*. The kids are with us the whole time, tired but not cranky. Most of the conversation is about the washing machine and what country it represents and the name of the English movie with the car. There's lots of discussion and disagreement and no conclusion, and no one cares.

At 2:30, Kathryn and I are the first to try to leave. We stand and offer to help clean but we're *les invités* and no one will let us. The only help we can be is to leave and let them do what they need to so they can go to sleep.

It's the last good time Kathryn and I have together. A week later we drive to Caen, Bayeux, the Cotentin Peninsula, and the Normandy beaches, where we do to each other what the Americans, French, British, and Canadians did to the Germans. We finish the summer in a truce, me on the third floor, she on the second, I writing fiction, she writing poems, each of us getting the last word. For appearances, we maintain a front for Monsieur and Madame P and Sharon and Jean, knowing it isn't necessary and suspecting they already know. They're French—romantic, nostalgic, sentimental, and fatalistic. When it comes to love, there's nothing new under the sun. Everything is possible and nothing.

"C'est la vie."

Buying a House

A week before I'm due to return to California, Madame P knocks on the door and tells me she wants to show me something. She tells me this by taking my hand and leading me to her car, saying "Allez, allez," which I've already learned means, Don't think about anything else.

I know she's going to show me something beautiful or important, something I should see before I leave, because all summer she has made certain I saw, ate, smelled, touched, and heard what was *spécial* in Finistère, and that I appreciated it as much as she does.

I get into her car and buckle up. She reaches over and checks to make sure I've done it right. Then she pulls out of her drive-way like she's entering the Grand Prix, and we're off to wherever we're going. All the way she talks to me as if I'm retarded, repeating words, using her hands—*both of them!*—gesturing, grimacing, encouraging, hoping, for her sake more than mine, that I learn the difference between *vingt* (twenty), *vin* (wine), and *vent* (wind); *cheval* (horse) and *cheveux* (hair); and *pêche* (fishing), *pêches* (peaches), and *péché* (sin) as fast as I can.

Thirty minutes later I see the sign, *Une Petite Ville de Caractère*, which is not an advertisement but an official ranking. The French rank everything: restaurants, hotels, water, roads, beaches, wine, each other, me—probably a remnant from the old days and their Cartesian belief in order, when they thought that the world still made sense and they could control it. We drive into the village, and it *is* beautiful, like Locronan, a combination medieval town and flower garden: bumpy cobblestone streets and fourteenth-century gray stone, yellow moss-covered buildings, every one covered with flowers. Begonias, fuchsias, and geraniums hang in pots and planters from windowsills, lampposts, fences, stone walls, the entire façade of the hotel de ville and the *poste*. Manicured flower boxes are in front of every shop and line the road. Also along the road and in public and private gardens are the largest, brightest, red, white, and blue hydrangeas and red, yellow, orange, pink, and white roses I've ever seen. It's a medieval fortress in bloom.

Madame parks in front of yet another thirteenth-century Breton chapel with another ornate Gothic spire and stark, scare-the-hell-out-of-me sculptures of saints and calvary. And in case I still haven't gotten the hint that this is for real and forever, there's an ossuary, which thankfully this time is full of old living and moving bones selling post cards instead of old dead bones turning to dust. I sit in the car and oooh, and ahhh, and mean it. The setting explains the Crusades and the Inquisition and all those French Huguenots living in St. Louis and Quebec.

We get out of the car and I begin "c'est joli-ing." The town, "c'est joli," the flowers, church, gardens, people, the tea we have, cookies—galettes—all are "C'est joli." I know *joli* means pretty, but I pronounce it and hear it as "jolly." The jam is jolly. The bread. Sky. Fish. Cows. Car. Everything is jolly—especially the rolling land dotted with huge rounds of hay and the heather-filled countryside; the skies and clouds and storms and rainbows; the texture and fabric of it all—small, sturdy granite houses with slate or thatch roofs, green lawns, geraniums and hydrangeas blooming everywhere, all under blue skies or gray skies or black skies filled with an illuminating light. It's enough to make me believe in elves and leprechauns, something I haven't done in forty years. I could almost, but not quite, reread *The Hobbit*.

As we walk back to her car, Madame asks me if I like the village. She asks me this by smiling, doing a 360, and holding out her arms like St. Francis talking to the sun. "Oui," I say, "c'est joli . . ." and I add the sentence that will change my life. "Mais je prefer Plobien. C'est magique."

I say it because I can and because it's true. With the river meandering outside our door like it's on permanent vacation, the salmon leaping out of the water to say "Bonjour," the two swans who became four, the heron, and all the sailboats—French, English, Dutch, German, moving upriver and down—the greenery, lush like Ireland, it is a startling, striking, beautiful, place; *spiritual* even, a word I rarely use now that the true believer, holier-than-thou, born-again Christian right has taken it over and all but disgraced it.

We drive back to Plobien, Madame chatting, me nodding, "Bonne-ing" and "Oui-ing" all the way. When the river comes into view, I smile, point at the sailboats, and say it again. "C'est joli. C'est magnifique. Magique. Incroyable." Madame looks at me for a long time, swerves to avoid wiping out a family of Brits on bikes, and says, "C'est vrai?"

I don't know what she means, but I can tell from the tone of her voice I'm supposed to say yes, so I do. "Oui."

"Bon," she says.

"Oui. Bon."

The next thing I know I'm standing in front of the bulletin board of the local real estate agent, who is called a *notaire*. The board is covered with photos of houses. Beneath each photo is a description I can't read and a price I can. Madame points at the board and says something. I understand two words, *vous* and *achetez*—you buy. From the look on her face, I see she's serious, like, If you love it here so much, buy something. For some reason, it's a moment of truth: have I been telling it or not? I really like it here or I don't. I love you like I led you to believe, or I'm a shit.

I look at the photos, look at the prices, try to read the descriptions, give up, and point to four houses in the range of 450,000 to 550,000 francs: $75,000 to $85,000. Who knows why? I have less than $5,000 in the bank. I rent a one-bedroom apartment in Oakland for $800 a month and drive an eighteen-year-old Volvo I paid $1,500 for, the single most expensive purchase I ever made in the forty-seven years of my life. Madame says "Bon" and makes the sign of an X over one of my choices because of the owner, location, color, size, garden, roof, neighbors, smell—I don't know—and leads me back to the car.

It's almost noon, *midi*, the sacred hour, lunch, thankfully, time to go home. She turns the car in the opposite direction, and I realize I'm about to go house hunting in France. I have no money, don't speak the language, and I'm leaving in five days. As little as I know about real estate, this doesn't seem right. Nor does driving to the house without a phone call or appointment, but she's French, Breton, and has lived in this village for thirty years, knows everyone and every place, so I follow. What else can I do—she's driving!

We stop at the first house, which is shuttered and vacant. It's on a hill overlooking the river in Loscoat, a detached two-story house made of brick and a concretelike stucco with a few trees, a flower and vegetable garden, patio, about an acre of land, wraparound white plastic fence, and a full view of the river. I nod to Madame and smile, happy, amazed I could even contemplate affording something like this. In California the price of this house wouldn't buy me a garage or a fully equipped Mercedes. Madame says "Non."

"No?"

"Non."

"Pourquoi?"

She says something I don't understand. I shrug. She breaks a branch off the nearest tree, hunches up, and slowly makes her way up the stairs to the house. I get it: too many stairs. When I'm old I won't be able to live here—or someone, probably she, will have to carry me and she's telling me now she won't do it. Later I found out she didn't want me to buy in Loscoat because the taxes are much higher. Plobien is designated petite, agricultural, low-income, low-employment—the U.S. equivalent of protected property and restricted use.

We drive to the next house, which is attached, part of a row of houses, like Chez Sally. It's cheap, a deal, right on the quay, facing the river, in the center of Plobien, near the *mairie*, church, and the *poste*. It's also shuttered and unoccupied. I can't see much of anything, except that it clearly has been uninhabited for a long, long time, and it needs plenty of work. There are fix-me-uppers and fix-me-uppers, but this was like Warsaw after the war. Given my French, having read Peter Mayle, not knowing what work, labor, and material cost, not to mention that I have no money, and knowing it could be an open sore, a wound that never closes, and remembering the stories Madame told about the river flooding and salmon the size of Volkswagens swimming in her living room, I decide to let this one pass.

We get back in the car and head home. Madame turns the radio on so she won't have to talk to me. I'm relieved. My word has been tested, and I passed the test. I made the effort and looked for a house. It just didn't work out. "C'est dommage, c'est dommage. Je suis désolé." I try to sound like my heart is broken and I've lost my fondest wish, but I'm delighted. What the hell would I do with a house in France?

This is what I'm thinking when we drive past Madame and Monsieur's house. It's also what I'm thinking when we pass Chez Sally. At the *mairie*, Madame veers left onto the one-lane country road I've been walking twice a day. The road hugs the river, and as far as I know, dead-ends. I walk it in the daytime to watch the fields of wheat changing color with the light, sailboats moving up- and downriver, cows grazing, and salmon leaping for joy. At night, I see streaking meteors and shooting stars and constellations I've seen only in planetariums. I walk as far as the viaduct, a huge Roman-looking structure of hand-cut rectangular granite stones, built in 1866. The first time I saw it I was astonished. *Every* time I see it, I'm astonished. It's megalithic, and I wonder who would build a *stone* bridge four football fields long three years before the Brooklyn Bridge was begun? It's at least fifteen stories tall, with twelve arches connecting one side of the valley to the other, all so a tiny one- or two-car commuter train that looks like the Little Engine That *Hoped* It Could can cross the river. We drive under one of the arches and Madame toots her horn, which echoes all the way to the other side, to an area called Kostez Gwer, where I've never been, and stops in front of a house hidden by a cluster of bushes and trees.

I get out of the car and look around. All I can see is a detached house on about three-quarters of an acre of land, across the street from a small park facing the river. Two sail-boats idle near the quay. I cross the street to the river and see the lock, *l'écluse,* and think: location, location, location. Every boat has to sail in front of the house. Madame stands next to me as the two boats, one flying the French flag and the other the English, move forward into the lock. Both families wave to us. The French boat is shipshape, neat, *propre,* spiffy right down to perfectly coiled ropes and shiny decks. The Brit boat has clothes—*underclothes,* bras the size of balloons, panties like skiffs, skimpy briefs, and long johns—hanging from the rigging like clotheslines, all blowing in the wind, drying. The difference between the French and the English, proper ver-sus practical. Madame inhales sharply, making that whistling sound that tells me she takes the English boat as a personal affront mocking everything French, and also as confirmation of everything she knows about the Brits and cleanliness and Chez Sally. Once again, proof of biological casting and the great French naturalist Lamarck.

I walk along the quay trying to see the house, but most of it is hidden by a thicket of small trees. The lawn is cut, and there's a car in the driveway—so the house is occupied, and maybe even kept up. I cross the road to get a better view and am surprised to see it's an old stone house made of granite and slate woven together like a fine Harris tweed of tans, blues, black, grays, and rust. It is the kind of house—old, stone, lonely, a survivor—I've been admiring and ogling all summer. Sometimes they look medieval, like there ought to be a moat around them. Other times, like now, in the sunlight, they are wavy patches of light: silver, gray, white, blue, twinkling and winking, seemingly as surprised as I am that they're still here. And with good reason. Most of them have been torn down or have tumbled down, or the stone has been covered by a thick, white, stuccolike concrete for the same reason people in the 1950s painted their oak and maple furniture: to make it look more classy and refined and finished, less natural and raw. The house is a find, the only old, stand-alone, exposed-stone house on the quay.

That's what I'm thinking when Madame walks past me, pushes the driveway gate open, and walks down the driveway. I'm aghast. I want to hide. Even I, a renter-for-life, know this is a no-no: do not disturb the occupants. I start to walk back to the car when I hear her call, "Marc."

Merde. I walk back and stop at the gate. She's at the front door and she's going to knock. Holy *merde*.

She knocks.

No one answers.

Good. *Bon.* I hope no one comes to the door so I can leave, satisfied I gave it my best, upheld my word, and proved my worth. She knocks louder and calls out something that sounds like "Cuckooo, cuckoooo," which is exactly how I feel. In the U.S., I'd be afraid of being shot. Here, I'm afraid of ridicule.

A man finally opens the door and peeks out. His shirt is half in, half out. He looks perplexed and annoyed. It's one o'clock in the afternoon, and he's either been doing something very important or napping. I can't tell if he's tired, angry, or bored. For the first time in my life I feel like a Jehovah's Witness.

Madame begins talking to him. I can't hear her, but I know she's talking because of the expression of dismay on his face. He says something back. She says something else. Clearly, she wants in, and he doesn't want to let her. I stand at the gate, waiting, knowing the poor guy doesn't have a chance. After a few minutes, she turns around, calls "Marc," and waves me over.

I shuffle down the path like a dead man walking and stop and stand behind Madame. Monsieur is barefoot and curling his toes. I have no idea what this means, but neither one is speaking, and this is France, so I know it's not good. I can't tell if they know each other and don't want to talk, or if they don't know each other and don't want to talk. I later learn they know *about* each other, as does everyone else in the village: names, lives, problems, failures, fortunes, illness, success; what people eat; when they drink; who they sleep with, but they don't actually know each other and have never formally met, which is common. As egalitarian as France likes to think it is, people from different backgrounds do not socially mix. I, however, a helpless stranger in a strange land, have brought my neighbors together, either from their natural, native goodwill, their *savoir-faire*, or their fear of being prosecuted under France's tough Good Samaritan Law, which requires them to offer assistance in an emergency—and to any reasonable French person, I'm an emergency just waiting to happen.

Madame introduces me. "Marc. C'est Monsieur Nedelec."

I don't know what to do. He obviously doesn't want to see us now, and he doesn't want to show his house. He holds out his hand like an American and says "Hello."

I shake it and doubtfully ask, "Parlez vous anglais?" I once waited three hours for a tour of a château because I was told it would be conducted in English and I'd enjoy it so much more.

The guide said "ahlo" and "good-bye," that was it. Since then, whenever I'm addressed in English, I don't assume anything, I ask. "You speak English?"

"Yes. Of course."

"Bon."

"You're a writer?"

"Yes," I say, and wonder what else Madame told him.

"Américain."

"Oui."

"You're leaving in a week?"

"Oui, oui."

"The house is not clean. My wife is not here. I will show you quickly, if you like."

I look at Madame, shrug, and say "Bon."

He opens the door and I walk in. Madame stays put. The change inside the house is palpable. Outside, it is bright, sunny and hot—unseasonably hot in the high eighties—but inside, in the front hallway, the house is dark, cool, refreshing. It's like walking into an air-conditioned theater on a hot sunny day, only this isn't air-conditioning, it's what happens when you have three-foot-thick granite walls.

I follow Monsieur over a brown-and-ocher star-patterned tile floor that I find out later is early twentieth century, up the stairs, past the first-floor landing to the second, the attic, which is startlingly bright. It has three skylights and is huge, running the entire length and width of the house, and jam-packed full with cartons, newspapers, a mattress, box spring, books, papers, and clothes. Bisecting the room diagonally is either a wire clothesline or a garrote. "We don't use this very much," he says.

No kidding. The ceiling is an A-frame that peaks at under six feet in the center and drops to less than two at the sides.

Hundreds, maybe thousands of long rusty nails poke through the roof, making the room some sort of medieval torture palace and a haven for tetanus, a shot I haven't had in thirty years. To my right, I see a sink so stained and spotted it looks like it has leprosy. Monsieur sees me looking at it and pulls a string hanging from a single light bulb in the center of the room to show me the room has electricity. Then he turns the light off and leads me down the stairs to the first-floor landing, where there are four doors, all shut. He points to two on the opposite side of the landing. "That's the toilet, and that's the bathroom." Then he opens the door to his left for me to look in. It's dark, like a cave, the shutters are closed and no lights are on. I'm unable to see a thing.

Monsieur leads me down the stairs, back to where we started at the front hallway. He points to the right, showing me the kitchen, letting me know I am not to enter. It has a large window facing the river and a red rose bush in bloom, the same turn-of-the-century tile floor as the hallway, a beamed ceiling, and old, dark-wood paneling that looks as if it came from a church, covering what once was a huge, stone cooking fireplace. Monsieur turns me left and points me into a small dark room with a fireplace, beamed ceiling, hardwood floor, and beautiful granite-and-slate stone wall. It's like a miniature hunting lodge with its smell of smoke, burnt wood, maybe game, or an old library with its built-in bookshelves overflowing with books. It's nice, I think. I like this house. It has three floors, if you count the tetanus attic, plenty of room to live in and to write.

"There's one more room, if you'd like to see."

"Sure," I say, Mr. Polite.

He leads me through the dark library–game room, to the darkest spot, where I see a black door I hadn't seen before. It's less than five feet high and cut through the three-foot thick stone wall. He opens the door, and I trip over a step I don't see and fall into another world.

Facing me is a forty-foot-long wall of shimmering granite and slate bathed in light. Built into the wall are two huge— large enough to walk into—fireplaces, each one big enough to roast a pig. Between the fireplaces, a double window looks out at a five-foot-high slate wall that separates the rear of the house from an open field. I step into the room, gaga. To my left, forty feet away, is another stone wall of granite and slate with a window that looks at the yard and a strand of thirty-foot-high cypress trees more than one hundred feet away. The wall to my right is white plaster and has a window that looks onto more yard, a stone shed, and another strand of thirty-foot cypress trees at least one hundred fifty feet away. The ceiling has four skylights, beams, and a double cathedral roof in the shape of an M, peaking twice at twenty-five feet. The floor is terra-cotta tile. In the middle of the room, forming a perpendicular, are two old, bent wooden beams. One runs the width of the room, at the bottom of the M, to brace the roof. The other runs from the crossbeam to the floor. I later learn Plobien was a working port until the 1950s, and every home along the quay was also a café, which is why this room was added onto the house. That's why there are two steps to enter the room and two fireplaces, and why the interior wall separating this room from the small dark room is three-foot-thick granite and slate instead of quarter-inch plywood.

Monsieur starts walking, leading me out. I look around to take it all in, already picturing myself here, La Fontaine, Chateaubriand, medieval feasts with goblets, banners, shields, and family crests; a long wooden table covered with pheasants and game, stained with wine and candle wax; full-bosomed wenches everywhere. I see Bloomsbury, Antibes, a garden room, trellises with ivy growing up the walls, lots of wicker and wrought iron, big floppy hats, frilly dresses, and linen suits à la the twenties, Scott and Zelda. As I leave the room, three sheep are grazing in the field out back.

Out front, Monsieur tells me the house will be clean tomorrow and his wife, who speaks better English, will be there. "Come back tomorrow at three if you like."

I go back to the car where Madame, never one to waste a second, is crocheting. She looks up when I open the door, not missing a stitch. I rock my hand back and forth, *comme ci, comme ça*. I know I should tell her I don't have any money— but then why did we look at the other two houses and why did I point out this one, and what am I doing here, living the good, carefree, rich-looking American life? I have only one way to honorably put an end to this. I turn my hand into a telephone and say, "Ce soir je telephone les États Unis."

"Bon," Madame says. "Bon," I say, and she drops me at Chez Sally, ready to call the French Welcome Wagon. I go in and forget about it for the rest of the day, until Madame knocks on the door and turns her hand into a telephone. I shake my head no, and she looks like I kicked her dog, stole her bread, ate her tomatoes, and cut her roses. I tap my wrist, which doesn't have a watch, hold up one finger, and say "Une heure," and go back to reading *The New Yorker*. Then at three o'clock, 9:00 a.m. in New York, when she's likely to be out, I do what every self-respecting, independent baby boomer who wants to buy a house or needs an excuse does. I call my mom, collect.

"Hi, Mom."

"How are you, dear?"

"Fine, fine. I'm having a wonderful summer. This place

is beautiful." I tell her about the sailboats and the river, the incredible light, Monet and Matisse, Signac and Gauguin, all of whom lived and painted in Brittany, the leaping salmon, the northern California–like coast, Madame P and her family, everything. I even ask about relatives I don't know and listen when she answers. When there's nothing else to say, I say it.

"Ma, you won't believe this, but I think I found a house in France I want to buy."

I'm waiting for Are you crazy, nuts, what's the matter with you? "That's nice, dear," she says.

That's nice. Holy shit! Doesn't she get it, the code for Get me out of this! Stop me! I have to raise the ante.

"Well, the thing is I can't do it without help on the down payment, probably ten thousand." That'll do it, giving me money, even a loan, which she knows she'll never get back, to buy a house in France. Ha.

"Okay."

"Okay?"

"Sure."

"Really?"

"Why not?"

I don't get it. No Have you thought about this? or Did you check the roof, floor, foundation, heater, water, weather, gas, electricity; for leaks, cracks, breaks, bugs, fire, water, heat, or cold damage? Nothing. She asked me more questions when I borrowed (and never paid back) two hundred dollars to buy a suit when I got married.

My plan to tell Madame I couldn't get a loan was falling apart. Of course, I could lie and say I couldn't get the money, something I regularly do in the U.S., but for some inexplicable reason I want to do what's right, which means no lying. *Ce n'est pas propre.* Everyone I've met has done right by me.

I want to do the same with them. It's one of the things I like about being in France, it brings out the best of me, and always surprises me—and even when I think it won't be good for me, it is. It's a lesson I forget and relearn every day.

The next day I go back to the house with a plan to knock ten thousand dollars off the asking price. Why? Because it's the way my family does business. I settle on ten thousand because it's large, round, and even. The plan is to follow my dad's tried-and-true used-car buying method. Every five years, when it was time to buy a new used car, Dad would line up the ads in *The New York Times*, and then he'd line up the family. Mom was assigned the interior, and my sister, the youngest, the tires. My brother got the exterior—body, paint, fenders, chrome. My job was to follow Dad around and repeat what he said in a voice loud enough for the neighbors to hear.

On the chosen day, we all pile into the old used car and drive to some godforsaken place because Dad was always certain we'd get a better deal in the country. "Less competition," he'd say, "less demand, lower price. That's capitalism for you."

We always arrive at the destination in a sudden, well-planned, stomach-flipping stop to show this is whimsy, and we haven't been heading here for the past three hours. Then we leap out of the car like the Keystone Cops and hover over the quarry like locust. Mom opens the door, always unlocked, peers in, shakes her head in dismay, and says, "The headliner is ripped (dirty, stained). The dash is cracked. Right front passenger seat needs fixing. Door panel is loose." Meanwhile, my brother circles the car, calling out scratches and dents. "Rear bumper, dented and rusty. Three-inch dent in passenger-side rear door. Holy shit [this is the one time we're encouraged to use bad words], the hood is totally wrecked." My sister walks around the car kicking the tires, saying things like "tread," "wear," and "uneven." She's too young to know what she's saying, but she says it very convincingly. I wait for Dad to go into action. He looks under the car and sees a dry oil patch. "Oil leak," he says. "Oil leaking all over the place," I yell. "Could be water too," he says. "Water too," I yell.

When the guy finally sees us and comes out—we never knock at the door, we wait for them to see us—he proudly opens the hood to show off what he has—350 horsepower, dual carbs, Webers, chrome manifold—Dad really starts in. "Really dirty engine. Corrosion around the battery. Looks like blow-by. When was the last tune-up?"

"The car's filthy," I yell. "Needs *lots* of work."

"Tires, too," my sister says.

"Interior."

"Body."

At which point, Dad asks about price.

This is how he bought two beach houses, a penthouse in Florida, two apartments in New York City, a '72 Stingray, '56 Thunderbird, and '68 Shelby Cobra, all at far below market price. It is also how I intend to lower the price of this house in France by ten thousand dollars, whether I buy it or not.

I knock on the door at the prearranged time, expecting the worst. If Monsieur is grave and not forthcoming, what would Mrs. Monsieur be like?

The door opens, and a dark, petite Liza Minnelli in *Cabaret* lookalike smiles at me and says, "Hello. Welcome. Come in," in *English* English. Standing behind her is Monsieur. He's dressed in black pants, a gray shirt, and polished loafers, and he's looking me over carefully. Madame leads me into the kitchen to the table, on which sit a glass vase of dried flowers, a white teapot, and three black cups. "Sit down," she says, pointing to the chair facing the window, looking out at the trees, the blooming red rose bush, and the river, where two swans float by as if on cue, and pours me a cup of tea.

"You're a writer?" she asks. Monsieur doesn't say anything. A sailboat glides upriver. I'm suspicious. This could be the normal way French people do business, and it could be a trick: drink tea, make small talk, get friendly, butter me up, and take advantage. Dad told me about rural cunning. "These people may live in the boonies, but they're not dumb. Be careful." I decide to play along, answer their questions, and bide my time until it is time to deal. It isn't until months later that I realize this *was* the deal.

I tell them I write fiction, short stories, that I'm a college teacher, a professor, and that I'm American, not English, because I know it matters, and that my father emigrated to France from Hungary when he was a boy, and to the U.S. from Marseille after living in Strasbourg for several years in the 1920s, and that he'd recently died. Madame tells me she and Monsieur are Breton. She also tells me the house is an old farmhouse built in the 1870s, and they are selling it because they've recently been given a *very* old house from Monsieur's family that they want to fix up and live in, and it is too difficult to do from here. I like her. I feel *sympa*, though I'm not exactly sure what it means. We talk for almost an hour, none of it about the house. Finally, after three cups of tea, Monsieur says something in French. She laughs. It's the first time I've seen him happy.

"Voilà," she says, "Would you like to see the house?"

"Sure," I say. "Oui."

Madame stands, I stand, Monsieur stands, and in that order we march up the stairs. "The stairs are old," she says, "original to the house." I immediately begin looking for loose boards, cracks and chips in the wood, blemishes of any price-reducing sort, but I don't see anything. The lights are all off and the shutters half closed—and I wonder what they're hiding. The walls need paint and so does the banister. It's impossible to see what else. It needs light fixtures.

We turn on the first-floor landing and head up the stairs to the attic. I'm surprised they've made no attempt to fix it up, make it look like a kid's room or a study or nook. It looks exactly as it did yesterday, a long, sloped, low-ceilinged dumping ground filled with clothes, a mattress and box spring, papers, books, and the clothesline/garrote. The lightbulb hanging from its wire in the middle of the room looks like a hanged man. Behind it, under the skylight and against the wall, is the leprosy sink. "Is there water in the sink? *Hot*, running water?" I ask, ringing one up for Dad.

Madame looks at Monsieur, then walks to the sink and touches it—something neither Monsieur nor I have the courage to do—and turns the faucet. Water sputters, pours, steams forth. "Voilà!" She points to the floor. "The wood is original, but unfinished." I look at it. The floor is primitive, ten-inch-wide, half-inch-thick, rustic-cut planks of white pine. I'm in trouble. Yesterday I saw this room as a horror chamber and a personal-injury lawyer's delight. Today it represents the most dangerous word in the real estate buyer's lexicon—*potential*. I see a study, a writing place, my master bedroom with private bath. The bad news is it would take me years and a fortune to build. The good news is it will never happen.

Madame leads our procession back down the stairs to the first-floor landing, which has the same ten-inch-wide plank floors as the attic, only these are finished and stained dark cocoa brown. I happily note the hallway walls are dun and need painting. We turn left on the landing and Madame opens the door to the cave room. Monsieur reaches in and turns on a lamp with a 40-watt bulb. In the dusk-light I see loose wires for an overhead light fixture that's not there, a beamed ceiling at least twelve feet high, a fireplace, radiator—central heat?— a closed and shuttered window that must face the river, and the same original wood floor.

Monsieur turns off the lamp and closes the door. Madame leads us across the landing to the room on the other side of the stairs and stops in front of the closed door. "This is our bedroom," she says. "It's the same as the room you just saw," which I actually didn't. She opens the door and we're enveloped in light. I walk through the room, straight to the window—a moth to the light, or a sunflower?—and look out over the thicket of trees in the front yard, at the two swans in the river, the cotton-ball sky, evergreen hills, and the horizon. Then I turn around and look at the room. It needs paint, some plastering, and there's no overhead light fixture, but it's large and cozy at the same time: large because of the window and the light and the twelve-foot ceiling; cozy because of the fireplace, the beams in the ceiling, and the dark, cocoa-brown floor.

"I love the light here," I say. "I love the light."

"Yes," Madame says, "it's magic." Monsieur says nothing. I had no idea a French person could be so quiet. It must be some sort of trick. He closes the door when we leave.

Facing us, on the landing, are two more closed doors. I'm starting to feel as if I'm in a French version of *Let's Make a*

Deal—I'll take door number three. Madame opens the door nearest us and steps back for me to see the shiny white toilet sitting alone in a narrow, dark, windowless room with a twelve-foot ceiling, looking like an objet d'art, or a throne, or the electric chair. She closes the door, then opens the second one: the bathroom. It's as light as the toilet is dark. It has the same window as the bedroom, the same light and view of the trees, sky, river, and horizon. The room is blue—the Blue Room—navy blue carpeted floor, swirly royal blue and white tile walls, navy blue ceiling, with a big old white porcelain bathtub, a shower, a sink, a radiator, and a bidet. If I were in the U.S., I could stand in the shower luxuriating, look out the window, and be in the sky. But this is France, rural France, Brittany—the end of the world—and probably, like Chez Sally's and every other shower I've been in, the hot water will run out in ten seconds, and I'll freeze my nuts and hurry out. I note the ceiling needs painting and a few tiles around the side of the tub are missing. One of the panes in the window is cracked, and the radiator looks rusty and dangerous and probably doesn't work.

Monsieur takes over and leads the way down the stairs like he wants to get me over with as soon as possible. Madame follows him, and I follow her. At the bottom of the stairs he turns left, into the small, dark, library-reading-hunting room that he and I walked through yesterday with its built-in bookcases and gazillion books. He turns on the light, an overhead light, albeit a 60-watter, and I say, "I like overhead light," and he turns on another light, a sconce on the wall. In the far corner, I see a pink flowery couch and a fancy stereo system with speakers the size of a cow. Record jackets and cassettes are all around it, all kinds of music, classical, French, opera, chanteuse, world, jazz, blues, Arab, rock, country, much of it

American. . . . Monsieur may not say much, but he thinks, reads, and listens. Hmmmm.

"Do the fireplaces work? *All* of them?" I see amorous fires and candles and heavy red wine and oysters in winter—and using the bidet for something other than laundry or washing my feet. I have no girlfriend, lover, or prospects, but being in France fills me with hope.

"Yes," Madame says, "but we never use them."

"The radiators work?"

"Of course," Monsieur says, as if I accused him of being Belgian or trying to trick me and sell me a pig in a poke. "The house has central heating. Oil. I will show you."

He leads us through the cozy nestlike room, under the five-foot doorway, over the step, into the cathedral ceilinged, forty-foot-long stone medieval garden-party room and points out the window to the tiny stone shed. "The oil tank and heater are over there," he says. "Oil heats the radiators and all the hot water in the house."

I want to ask if everything works, how old it is, when it was last checked, how much it costs to heat, repair, replace, but I don't. I follow Monsieur as he walks us through the medieval garden-party room, to the other side, where he opens another five-foot door cut into the stone wall, and we're back in the kitchen.

Madame directs me back to "my" chair and pours me a cup of tea. Ha, I think, and start to go over my list: bedrooms, halls, the whole house really, needs painting and plaster repair; overhead wires are exposed; drainpipe is loose and not connected; chipped and missing tiles in the bathroom; worn and scratched wood; cracked window; rusty radiators; dingy shutters; the tetanus attic; and the garden needs work—not that I'd know it or do it, but gardens always need work so why not claim it? Before I can say anything, Madame says, "French law requires me to tell you everything about the house, and I will."

In the U.S., that sentence alone would trigger calls to lawyers, plumbers, engineers, electricians, roofers, architects, and exterminators. In France, I have no one to call, so I listen. Madame tells me the electricity is an old system and needs upgrading, and the drainpipe is loose. She says the rest is cosmetic—painting, plastering, sanding, polishing. They've taken care of everything else, including draining the septic tank, which I didn't even know existed. "Oh!" she adds, "We have extra tiles for the kitchen, bathroom, and back-room floors if you want them."

If I want them! She assumes I'm buying, which is not a good sign and goes directly against Dad's tried-and-true tell-them-what's-wrong-and-how-much-it-will-cost-to-repair-or-replace strategy. I'm about to say, What about the garden? And, Everything needs fixing up. It'll cost a fortune. The house has been on the market for months. It will never sell at this price. . . . And offer them $10,000 less. Why not? I don't have the money to pay either price, and saying all this will kill the deal. To this day, I don't know why I didn't say it or counter with a lower price. Instead, I said, "Do you mind if I walk through the house again?"

"Of course. Take your time."

I walk through each room, sit in each room. Feel it. Practice feng shui before I knew such a belief system existed. I move furniture, face it in different directions, touch the stone walls, look out the windows, open the skylights. I sit on a chair in the medieval garden-party room and look at the two fireplaces and granite and slate walls and see how the stone was recently pointed and set, how much work and love they've given the house. I see parties and pageants and my family here. I want it, which I know from Dad is the worst time to buy. But I feel it in my heart. I see myself here, in this house, this village, with these people, in Brittany. It's crazy, I know. Place has never been important to me. In my fiction, place—home, town, village, state—is rarely specified or identified. My characters hardly leave their heads or look out a window. What moves them is desire and love—fear of it, loss of it, attaining it, missing it, accepting it, wanting it. And love is always a person (someone to love you back if you're lucky), not an object or state of being or a place, but here I am wanting, desiring—*loving*—this place. The fact that it's six thousand miles from home, in another country, a country that speaks a language I don't understand, and that I have to fly ten hours to get here doesn't seem to matter a whit. What does matter, though, is that I still don't have a dime.

I went through this once before, two years earlier, in Wyoming. I spent two months in a village of twenty-five people about eighty miles north of Sheridan and never wanted to leave. Again it was the light, the sky, the space, the majesty, and the price. Houses could be bought for what people in California were paying for Hondas or trips to China. I looked at two places and wanted one badly, but finally decided against it for three reasons: (1) If I had a house in Wyoming, I would drive there, meaning it would take me three days to get there and three days to get back; (2) the food would be frozen and processed and junk; and (3) for entertainment I'd go to the neighborhood bar on weekends and get the shit beaten out of me for being too short or eastern or western or liberal or Jewish or hippie or Democrat or Green or antigun, pro-abortion, whatever.

France has none of these obstacles. I can go door to door, Oakland to Plobien, in twenty hours. As for food, it's France. The food is fresh, new, and delicious, eaten in season, à la Alice Waters. I can eat for a week—fresh oysters, Atlantic salmon, Breton lobster, langoustine, mussels, halibut; local farmer's chickens, eggs, butter, cheese, honey, pork; juicy apples and pears, sweet melons, vine-perfect tomatoes—all for less than the cost of a high-end dinner in San Francisco. And unless you're a chicken or a pig, violence and fear of violence are not factors in your life. (Fear of loathing, though, is something else.) If I get hungry or sick or lucky enough to be old, this is the place to be. It's crazy. I have no money, but I'm certain as I rarely am about anything that I want to be part of this house, this village, these people, and Brittany.

"Okay," I say, walking into the kitchen. "I'd like to make an offer."

They both look at me blankly.

"I'm interested. Now what do we do?"

"We agree."

"Who?"

"We."

"You and me?"

"Yes. Of course."

I explain to them how houses are sold in the U.S. Two real estate agents, inspectors, lawyers, banks, proof of this, assurance of that, insurance, fees, fees, fees, and points. They look horrified.

In France, the *notaire* represents both parties and is an official of the state. He's also a lawyer, banker, and a broker. His fee is fifteen percent of the sale, and the buyer—me—pays. He essentially makes a private agreement, a *compromis de vente*, public. He verifies that the village is not about to build a bridge over the house or a nuclear plant in the backyard, the seller has the right to sell the house and no distant cousin can claim it, and no neighbor has the right to run a herd of sheep or pigs through your living room once a year.

Madame walks me through the house again, making sure I've seen everything I need to see. We return to the kitchen and reach an agreement: they agree to fix the drainpipe, I agree to pay their price. It's the only time in France I paid more than fifty dollars for anything and didn't bargain. The only stipulation is the exchange rate. It's 6 francs to the dollar when we agree. If it falls below 5.7, I can call the deal off. The whole thing is contingent on my getting a loan, which is my out if I wake up in a day or month and want out. That's it, the whole deal. On my way out, I ask them to leave me what they don't need—as I have nothing—and regret it as soon as I say it, remembering the attic, convinced they'll leave all of it, and *I'll* have to clean it out.

I walk back to Chez Sally giddy, frightened, and perplexed. I've been in the house twice for a total of less than three hours, have had no inspections, no experts, only the word and guarantee of the owners that nothing is wrong. Six thousand years of shopkeepers, bankers, and lawyers and it's come to this. My father and his father and his father's father—all the way back to Egypt, Adam, and *Australopithecus* must be shaking their heads.

Two days later I'm sitting with Monsieur and Madame Nedelec in the *notaire*'s office, where he hands me a document to sign. I drop it on his desk and explain my scheme. Twenty percent of the price of the house is taxes. If we "lower" the price, I explain with a wink, the taxes would be less. I'd pay Monsieur and Madame their price and the *notaire* his fee, but I'd only have to pay the state 30,000 or 40,000 or 50,000 francs, and I'd save $5,000 to $10,000. They'd get their money and I'd save mine. *Quel deal!* I was finally doing right by Dad. I explain all this to the *notaire*, who doesn't understand a word I say. Madame Nedelec translates, and as she speaks, the *notaire* smiles, nods, taps his head with a finger to indicate I'm either smart or nuts, then when she finishes, he speaks, and she translates for me.

"It's illegal. He's an official of the state. He says to say this in front of him is a crime. You could be arrested." Holy shit! I'm going to jail with Papillon and Dreyfus. "Besides," she explains, "the transaction involves transferring large sums of foreign money and is easy to trace and impossible to hide." I take the document I can't read and sign it, committing me to buy a house when all I have is ten thousand dollars I borrowed from my mom. The *notaire* then writes a note and hands it to me. It looks like a high school pass to go to the bathroom. I look at him and Madame blankly.

"It's for the bank," she says.

"The bank?"

"Yes, you need it to open an account in France."

All of a sudden, this is becoming real. We're talking honest-to-God dollars or francs or whatever. I look at the document I just signed. At its best, it commits me to $85,000 for a house, fees, taxes, and whatnot, none of which I actually have. At its worst, who knows what penalties I've agreed to if the deal falls through. All I know is, they are all happy, and I'm scared out of my mind.

I take my copy of the document and the scribbled note and leave, bewildered. I go back to Chez Sally and show Madame P the document and the note. She reads it, confers with her husband and son, and acts as if all is correct. *C'est propre. C'est normal.* Then she takes my hand and says the word I've come to hate, "Allez." In the U.S. it's "Honey, we have to talk." In France, it's "Allez," because the result is the same: I'm about to lose control.

We get into her car, where she all but buckles me in. If there were a car seat, she probably would have sat me in it. She then proceeds to drive 100 kilometers an hour on a two-lane country road back to Loscoat. I've never gotten there so fast, though I still have no idea where we're going.

She parks the car and we get out, her holding my hand like the retard I've become.

"Où?" I say.

"À la banque."

"Bon. C'est joli."

We enter Crédit Agricole, a bank I've never heard of or been in. It looks to me like a fly-by-night operation, a Marx Brothers routine, a con: no security guard, no Plexiglas windows, no long lines, four tellers, all young, handsome, smiling, shaking their customers' hands. A bank for farmers, right! Me and the chickies and pigs. I figure it'll be gone in the morning. How could I know it's about to become the second-largest bank in Europe?

Madame, still holding my hand, pulls me up the stairs. In my other hand, clenched, is the scribbled note from the *notaire*. Madame P says something to the secretary and we sit and wait on a couch. In a few minutes a short, casually dressed, no suit, no tie, no jacket, slightly balding, eyeglassed man in his late fifties comes out of an office, gives Madame P the double-cheek kiss and shakes my hand, and we follow him into his office, the office with *Président* written on the door. At forty-seven years old, I've never in my life met or spoken with a bank president. Once, when I bounced a check, I spoke with a supervisor. And now here we are, Monsieur le Président, Madame P, and I, sitting, she and I facing him, in his simple, comfortable, proper office—which feels to me like the principal's office in high school—doing what?

"Hello," says Monsieur le Président.

Madame turns to me, smiles, and says, "Il parle bien anglais."

Shit! Now I'm really in trouble. Sure enough, that's the last English word I hear, unless of course you count *monnaie*. Madame P begins speaking, looks at me, and shrugs, once again astonished, I think, at how someone so helpless could still be alive. Monsieur le Président is saying, "Oui, oui, bien sûr," and looking at me. I'm clutching the paper the *notaire* gave me as if it is a get-out-of-jail card or a prescription for ampicillin.

Monsieur le Président begins writing, filling out forms. When he finishes he gives the papers to Madame P, who gives them to me to sign. Why not? I've already agreed to buy a house I can't afford. I sign. As soon as I do, he says something else I don't understand. I look at Madame. She says something that sounds similar to what he just said. I look at Monsieur le Président. Madame stands and pats my wallet, which is in the torn rear pocket of my jeans. I take it out and hand it to her, thinking she wants a driver's license or Social Security card, some piece of real identity. She removes two $100 traveler's checks, puts them on the desk, and hands me a pen, indicating I should sign them. What's this? Some secret French fee? A version of French points that no one bothered to tell me about? A kickback? A payoff? What? I don't know, I'll probably never know, but I sign, kissing those two hundred dollars good-bye.

Madame gives the two checks to Monsieur le Président, who begins filling out more forms. Five minutes later he finishes and hands me a booklet with "Crédit Agricole" on the cover. I open it and see I now have a checkbook and a checking account in France with two hundred dollars' worth of francs in it. That's it. I stand up, thinking we're finished. I sit down, seeing we're not. Monsieur le Président wants to discuss the house, the mortgage, a loan, *monnaie*. He met me fifteen minutes ago. He knows nothing about me—am I a nut, a loony, employed, employable, do I have income, savings, prospects, anything?—and he's offering me a loan to pay for the house. I can't believe it. I can only attribute it to Madame P, who seems to have the powers of Aladdin. I didn't know then that getting a loan in France is easy. It's getting the bank account that's hard, but nothing compared to getting a telephone. I thank him and turn him down, not wanting to pay the daily fluctuating exchange rate for the next fifteen or twenty years, possibly doubling the cost of the house. Besides, I want to get the loan in the U.S., where two out of five of the tellers in my local bank speak English.

Two days later I leave France with a French checkbook I don't know how to use, a written agreement that I can't read to buy a house, committed to spending $85,000 that I don't have. It doesn't bode well for international relations.

As soon as I get back to the U.S., I do three things. I call my mom to verify it was she who agreed to loan me $10,000 and not the wrong number or my sister playing a practical joke. I ask my friend Peggy to do a real translation of the *compromis* to determine the number of ways I've been cheated. And I visit the Alliance Française to inquire about French lessons.

When I determine it really was my mom and everything in the *compromis* is exactly as it was explained to me, I set about the task of getting money. Real money. Serious money. Dollars. As a socialist member of the downwardly mobile, propertyless middle class, this is something I've never done. Basically, I'm a pay-cash-or-borrow-from-Mom-have-no-debt kind of guy, so I think it's going to be easy, certainly as easy as it appeared to be in France. Ha.

Ha, ha, ha.

In France, you need a note from everyone you know to open a bank account, but once opened, getting money is a snap. In the U.S, it's the reverse. Anyone with five dollars in his pocket can open a bank account, but trying to parlay that into something else is a joke—on you!

I go to every bank in the Bay Area, including Crédit Lyonnais and Bank of the West, which at the time is French owned. Every one of them is willing to loan me up to one million dollars for a business in Europe, but not a nickel for a house.

"Why not?" I ask the twenty-something behind the desk. "What's the difference between a business and a home?"

"A business has inventory, sales, income. It's a better investment."

"A home has property, a building, two buildings, and I'm going to rent it for income. Isn't that a business—a B-and-B?"

Her answer was the same as everyone's, a smile, a shake of the head, and a "No."

That leaves me with two options: Monsieur le Président and a fluctuating, changing, diminishing dollar every day for the next twenty years, or Mom.

"Mom, hi, how are you?"

"Fine, dear, fine, and you?"

I intend to make small talk and work my way into the conversation. "I can't get a loan, Ma. No bank will lend me money for a house overseas."

"How much?"

"Seventy-five thousand."

"When?"

"By January." It's now October.

"Okay. Dad and I helped your brother and sister, so why not you?"

I've been teaching since I was twenty-four, have no debts, live within my means, and I need money from my mom to buy a house—and I'm no different from anyone I know, except my house is in France and everyone else's is in Oakland, San Francisco, Chicago, or New York. All of us, in our forties and fifties, still depending on our parents, a generation of downward mobility and lowered expectations. I cannot afford to buy anything in the Bay Area in the early 1990s, where the average price of a house is already over $300,000, but I can in France. And in a certain way it feels like a circle closing, roots, a coming home. After my father died, my mother, brother, sister, and I looked through old photos from Dad's family album, at his mother's and father's uncles and nephews, dark-eyed men no one can identify anymore, decked out in the formal World War I military uniform of France. My family.

From the moment Mom agrees to give me the money, I'm racked with doubt. What the hell am I doing? This is crazy, nuts, a lunatic idea. I hardly know these people—I *don't* know these people!—and as Kathryn had been so fond of saying, "If they knew what you were saying, if they understood you, believe you me, they wouldn't like you." I believed her. After all, it was certainly true of her. The more she heard me, the less she liked me. Why should France and French people be different? The farther I get from France, Brittany, the summer, and the people, the less and less it makes sense, and the more I want out.

The good news is I have that clause: If the dollar drops below 5.7 francs, I can get out. Every day, first thing, like some sort of tycoon, I go to the business section of the *San Francisco Chronicle*, a section I'd always used to line the garbage pail, to see how much the dollar has fallen. In two months, it drops from 6 to 5.5. Every day I look at the number, turn on my calculator, and determine how much I've lost. Meanwhile, I'm waiting for the money from Mom. I can't buy francs without her dollars, and she doesn't want to sell her stocks until she gets her price. So while she's making money, I'm losing it, big time. It's capitalism at its best.

When the dollar falls to 5.3 francs, the cost of the house increases $7,000, and for the first time, really, I think about abandoning it. What stops me is my dad. My entire childhood and teenage years he lamented the beautiful piece of property in the mountains he didn't buy because the owner wouldn't lower his price $3,000. With each telling, the $3,000 became worth less and less and his loss seemed greater and greater. "I should have bought it," he repeatedly said. He said it in a way that meant it would have changed his life if he had. Maybe, maybe not, I don't know, but I do know *I* don't want to be saying that for the rest of my life over a measly $7,000, which over twenty years amounts to $350 a year. Besides, I can always sell.

Finally, in January, with the dollar hovering around 5.4, Mom sends me a cashier's check for $75,000. I've never seen anything like it. The only number I've ever written that had three zeros had the decimal point to the left of two of them. I immediately put it in the bank and begin thinking about transferring it, getting it from the U.S. to France.

With the $10,000 down payment I used Bank of the West because it was French owned and I was feeling very Francophilic: anything French was good. It was also easier to transfer the money, but the one thing it wasn't was cheap. The fees were high and the exchange rate was low. It was not a good deal for me. It was the price of safety and convenience, I thought. But for $75,000—and with the dollar at 5.3—I need the best rates possible. I ask friends, check the phone book, call around the Bay Area, and finally find a place with an 800 number that offers me an incredible rate.

I'm thrilled and immediately suspect. Who are these guys? It's 1992, before the Internet, and research is not so easy. Still, I do what I can. I call every day, morning, noon, night, weird hours and weekends, using different names and asking the same questions, trying to catch them in a slip-up. Someone always answers the phone—money never sleeps— and always has the right answer, or at least the same answer. I latch on to a guy named Gary, or a guy who calls himself Gary, or tells *me* his name is Gary, and it feels as if I'm dealing with *someone*, even though I know I'm not. I feel like the unknown third Hunt brother, and I'm hoping the same thing doesn't happen to me. The entire exchange is done over the phone and through the mail. I don't have a cell phone, ATM card, or debit card. I still go *into* the bank, talk to the tellers, hand them a check, and wait for my cash and paper receipt— and I *wire* a $75,000 cashier's check to a guy named Gary whom I never met, at a bank in Utah, where, Gary swears, they will wire 400,000 francs to my Crédit Agricole account in France. All I can think of is *The Sting*. I cannot believe

I'm giving $75,000 to someone I never met and wiring it to a place I've never been on the assurance of a stranger named Gary. The moment I wire the money, I'm certain I'll never see it again.

In February I fly back to France for the closing—with my mom. I feel like a jerk, a middle-aged man traveling with his mother. But as soon as we land, I'm relieved. Mom speaks French. Understands French. Can read French. All of which means we find our luggage, the car rental desk, and our way out of Paris.

It's cold and wet and there's snow on the ground—it's beautiful. We spend two nights in Rouen, where Joan of Arc was burned, two nights in Honfleur, where Erik Satie died, and a night in Saint-Malo, which was destroyed by Allied bombing and rebuilt after the war.

It's raining when we leave Saint-Malo and still raining, a light drizzle, when we enter Finistère. The clouds are woolly, not solid or dense as they were in Rouen and Honfleur. There's no snow. The land is hilly, rolling, lush, dark green, accentuated by black slate walls, tree windbreaks, and hedgerows. "It's like Ireland," Mom says repeatedly. "It's magical."

"Almost there," I say, and I swear, as we exit the N165, a rainbow breaks out and the pot of gold is in Plobien.

I drive past the house to show it to Mom and my stomach sinks. It's dark, bleak, shuttered, and closed, looking lonely and unused, uninhabited and uninhabitable, leaving me scared and embarrassed. I brought her all the way here and borrowed all that money for this. Mom says nothing. I want to apologize. I'm so sorry about everything, from wanting the house and borrowing the money to asking the owners to leave me what they could, certain I've bought an old dilapidated house filled with junk.

We drive to Chez Sally, which I've rented so we'd have a place to stay before the closing, whenever that is. It's clean because Kathryn and I were the last ones there. I open the door and Mom frowns. The house is clean, but it's been shut for five months, so it's cold, damp, dank, and it smells. I know what Mom's thinking, because I'm thinking it too. Thankfully, she says nothing.

We silently unpack and try to settle in, but it quickly becomes apparent that the baseboard electric heat is worthless and the house is freezing and will never, no matter what, short of a major conflagration, be warm or dry. We bundle up in the long johns, sweaters, boots, heavy New York winter coats, scarves, gloves, and hats we brought and start to straighten things up for our next month. I attempt a fire, but the fireplace is too small and doesn't draw. The whole time we're doing this I'm wondering about my house, the heat, warmth, fireplaces, dampness, smell, no inspections, tests, engineers, experts, and I'm fearing the worst. In my heart of hearts, I know I've been duped.

We eat a can of soup for dinner and go to bed early, Mom to the second-floor bedroom, me back to the third, both of us freezing and exhausted, at least one of us very depressed.

The next morning I'm the first person at the bank. The door opens at exactly nine o'clock. I walk up to the front teller, a boy who looks sixteen, and say, "Bonjour, Monsieur," and shake his hand like I'm a regular. Then I hand him the piece of paper with the name of the teller Monsieur le Président gave me five months ago and point to the name, then to the floor, and say, "Ici?" Here?

The kid doesn't even blanch. He walks to the back of the bank and returns with a girl who looks fifteen. I don't have a prayer, I know it.

"Yes, hello, Mr. Greenside, may I help you?" She holds out her hand to shake.

I'm astonished. She speaks perfect English with an English accent. I shake her hand, hoping she never gets older, marries, has kids, or moves away. Then I hand her my checkbook and ask about my account. "Did the money I wired arrive?"

She taps the computer keyboard, taps some more, then some more, and says, "When did you send it?"

"Several weeks ago."

"It's not here."

"No?" I'm dumbfounded, incredulous.

"No."

"Where could it be? It was a lot of money. I need it to buy a house."

She taps some more. "It's not here." She doesn't seem worried or concerned, like the bank screwed up and it happens all the time or she's humoring me. Either way I'm lost. Fifteen minutes ago I felt like J. P. Morgan. Now I feel like Ralph Cramden. I thank her and race to Chez Sally to call Gary.

"Hi," Mom says. She's in the living room, bundled like an Eskimo, hovering over the electric heater, sipping her morning tea. "What's wrong?" I wave her away, not having the nerve to tell her. I find Gary's card and the Foreign Exchange invoice, which somehow I knew I would need, and dial Gary's personal number. A woman's voice recording answers telling me he's "not at his desk." It's eight hours later in France, making it 2:00 a.m. in Utah—*if that's where he is*—no wonder he's not at his desk. I leave the number of Chez Sally and a message for him to call me. I hang up certain I'll never see my money again.

I begin calling Gary at noon while Mom is at Madame P's eating a warm lunch. At 1:15—5:15 a.m. Utah time—someone not Gary answers the phone. "Is Gary there?"

"He's not at his desk."

I explain that I'm calling from France, trying to buy a house, and have no money. "The money was supposed to be wired weeks ago and isn't here."

"Don't worry. I'll check. Give me your number and we'll call you back."

They don't, and I try not to panic.

The next day I'm the first person at the bank. I walk in and the sixteen-year-old-looking boy at the front desk says, "Bonjour Monsieur," shakes my hand, walks away, and returns with the fifteen-year-old-looking girl, who says, "Hello," shakes my hand, and tells me in flawless English my money hasn't arrived. I return to Chez Sally and begin seriously calling Gary. Each time I call, the same person answers, "Foreign Exchange," which in a way is consoling, but when I ask for Gary, "He's not at his desk." By the second day, the person goes out of his way to assure me Gary is there, in the office, and exists. The more he assures me, the more I'm not. Mom has discussed this with Monsieur and Madame P, who are not concerned. Mom wants to hire a lawyer.

On the fourth day, Gary calls. He's found the money. By mistake, they wired it to Corsica. Gary sounds pleased with himself, but the only things I know about Corsica aren't good. Napoleon was Corsican. Corsicans are like Sicilians, and neither is known for being friendly, generous, or returning money to strangers. I figure I'll never see the money again, or if I do, it will be attached to a bloody hand. Gary says, "We'll have it for you in a day or two," and hangs up.

I go straight to the bank to tell the girl. I want to put her at ease and let her know I'm not a loony, because the last few times I've seen her I've been distressed. As I finish telling her the story, the *notaire* walks in. He sees me, shakes my hand, and speaks. I look at the girl, who says, "He wants to sign the papers tomorrow." Great. I get to use one of the two phrases I've been practicing. "Je n'ai pas d'argent." I don't have any money. The *notaire* laughs. Either I said it wrong—said something else—or he thinks this is some sort of American Jerry Lewis custom, those funny people, always joking.

I ask the girl to explain what I said and to tell the *notaire* the money will arrive in a few days and we can meet then to sign the papers.

He shakes my hand and says, "Demain à deux heures."

We're doing it anyhow! At 12:00. *Midi.* Lunch time. I don't get it. I ask the girl.

"*Two* o'clock," she says. "Deux heures, deux heures, not douze heures."

I'm in trouble. I studied numbers so I wouldn't get cheated, and I can't tell the difference between twelve and two. And that's not the worst of it. Tomorrow I'm buying a house with less than $10,000 in the bank.

I race back to Chez Sally to call Gary. The same person who always answers answers, "Foreign Exchange." I ask for Gary, and he says, "He's not at his desk. Shall I take your number and have him call you back?" He says it as if he's never spoken to me before. I hang up.

The next day at two o'clock Mom and I and Monsieur and Madame Nedelec and her mom arrive at the *notaire*'s office. I know why my mom is here—she bought the house—but why is Madame? Dueling moms? My mom can beat up yours? I size up the two moms. They're both about five feet tall. Mine's dressed for the theater: pearl necklace and earrings, silk scarf, fur hat, tailored wool slacks, and a long, stylish, below-the-knees, chocolate-brown down coat, making her look like a bear. Hers is dressed for church: elegant black wool coat, black wool skirt, black shoes, gold hoop earrings, her dark hair pulled tight in a bun; she's thin, angular, birdlike. Looking at the two moms and thinking about where I am and what I'm doing, the church and the theater are perfect—and I wonder how they knew. Her mom says something in French to my mom, who responds, and the two moms begin chatting away, illustrating once again the universality of momness.

The *notaire* arrives, shakes everyone's hand, and ushers us into a tiny, cramped, nothing-fancy, a-little-on-the-shabby-side office that says either he's so strong and successful and important he doesn't need any stinking accoutrements, or he's a failure. He sits behind his desk like he knows what he's doing. We sit in chairs facing him. I figure this is the time to tell them I don't have any money. "I wired it weeks ago, but it's not here now."

Madame translates what I said to the *notaire*, or at least I think she does. "Bon," he says.

Monsieur and Madame say "Bon."

Her mother says "Bon."

My mother says "Bon."

All of them look content.

I can't believe we're going through with this. We're going to sign papers, transfer the property, and sell the house—*after*

I told them I have no money. It's a way of doing business I know nothing about. Monsieur le Président is willing to lend me thousands of dollars not knowing if I have a job, income, or am crazy. Monsieur and Madame Nedelec are selling me their house *knowing* I have no money in the bank, and the *notaire*, an official of the state whose job is to make sure everything is on the up-and-up, approves. No wonder the Coneheads say they're from France. My own bank, where I've banked for twenty years and bounced only one check, wouldn't even meet with me when I told them I wanted a loan appointment to buy a house in France. The cashier at Safeway asks for my ID every time I cash a check, even though I've been cashing checks at her counter for twenty years.

The *notaire* stands and shakes everyone's hand again, then sits and explains the process. Madame Nedelec translates. The *notaire* talks for ten minutes. Madame translates it into two sentences. "He's done a title search and listed it, and no one has made a claim. . . ."

"What does that mean?"

"It means the house is mine to sell, and no relative has made a claim to it. My mother is here to verify that." When she finishes, the *notaire* removes a twelve-page document from his briefcase and begins to read. After each paragraph, Madame Nedelec translates and summarizes, then she as the current owner, her mom as the previous owner, and I as the new owner write *Lu et approuvé*, read and approved, and initial each paragraph, with two out of three of us knowing what we're doing. My mom just shakes her head. I know exactly what she's thinking. My dad was a lawyer—a Philadelphia lawyer—we were all taught never, ever, under any circumstances, with the possible exception of a birthday card, to sign anything without having it vetted by someone, preferably a lawyer, but at least a professional, definitely a Jew. And here I am surrounded by Christians—*Catholics*—initialing a document I can't read and don't understand, in a language I'll never master, the whole thing being explained and translated by the person I'm buying the house from. The only saving grace in this whole process is I don't have the money, so what's to lose?

When we finish, the *notaire* gives each of us copies of the papers. I sign a bunch more papers I don't understand, don't give them any money, and they give me the deed and the keys to the house, and somehow I feel taken. Monsieur Nedelec hands me another set of keys and says, "For the car."

"What car?"

"Our car. We're going to buy a new one. You can have our old one." I'm dumbfounded. I thought I'd seen and heard everything, but I hadn't. "Now we can tell you the story. . . ."

Oh shit . . . I'm screwed.

"You know Kostez Gwer?"

"Yeah. . . . It's the name of the area the house is in."

"Do you know what it means?"

"No-o."

"It's Breton. *Gwer* means green. *Kostez* means side. You're facing the green side of the hill, Monsieur Greenside."

"You're kidding."

"No."

"We didn't want to tell you before today because we didn't want to influence your decision, but as soon as we heard your name we knew it was meant to be." He and his wife are smiling. I don't get it. I have their house and the keys to their car and they have nothing—and they're as happy as anyone could be. I'm happy too, and that worries me more than anything.

———

Mom and I drive to the house, Kostez Gwer, Chez Green-side, and unlock the door. I am highly expectant. This is my first house, and the people I bought it from just gave me a car, yet part of me—which part? American, Jewish, male, son of a lawyer, New Yorker, I don't know—still expects to be cheated, robbed, misused. I open the door with great trepi-dation, expecting the worst—to fail in front of Mom—and am greeted by shiny, spotless, gleaming floors. The tile is almost one hundred years old and looks like new. We walk through the house, Mom and I together, oohing and aahing: the wooden floors, including the stairs and the attic, have all been cleaned, waxed, and oiled. Later, when I do it myself, I realize what it means: sweeping, dusting, vacuuming, then getting on your knees with a pile of rags and a can of oil and rubbing every plank, every corner, foot, and square centime-ter of a three-story house. Your back aches, knees, arms, chest. It's painful, and the only way to do it. I didn't know that then, when I first walked in, only that they took good care, were proud of their work and their house and everything was beau-tiful—and now and as long as I own the house, it is my job to do the same. Later, when I thank them for the care they took, their thoughtfulness, the car, everything, Monsieur shrugs, and says, "C'est normal." Madame says, "C'est propre."

I marvel. In spite of myself, they are going to bring out the best in me.

They leave a stove and refrigerator—both working, which I find out later is not common. Houses are usually bought and sold without appliances—only a sink and toilet. They also leave a polished oak parquet table with two leaves and four chairs, a set of dishes for eight—none chipped or cracked—silverware, pots, and a frying pan. A full, operating kitchen.

They leave a double bed, mattress and box spring, and a walnut armoire in the bedroom. The attic is spotless. Even the stone shed is clean and organized, and the fuel tank has oil. I'm amazed. I walk through the house again and see all the overhead wiring has been completed and connected to overhead lights. I go outside to check, though I already know—the drainpipe, which had been separated from the spout, is back in place.

Clearly Monsieur and Madame love their house and take their duty and responsibility as homeowners and Bretons seriously. What passes between us is a trust, personal and cultural, which I try to acknowledge, honor, and hope I do not betray.

Everyone I know in the U.S. owns a house, but not one of them, from my parents' generation to my nephews and nieces, has any kind of relationship, except maybe for a while litigation, with the previous owners. Except me. Monsieur and Madame Nedelec have become some of my closest friends in Brittany. Indeed, in my life.

Three days later my money arrives. I know this because Madame P tells me. She knows because the boy at the bank calls her, giving her the job of explaining it to me. So much for confidentiality. That afternoon I go to the bank.

"Bonjour," I say, putting out my hand to shake, showing I'm a local who knows the rules.

"Bonjour," the girl says, and gives me a piece of paper to sign, which I do, as usual, not knowing what I'm doing. Then she gives me a new checkbook. I stand there, dumbfounded. I'm supposed to pay the *notaire* to close the deal, but I don't know how to write the check, what goes where, where to sign it, date it, write the sum, not that I could write it anyhow. I turn the checkbook around and ask her to write it for me. I feel like a grammar-school kid opening my first bank account. She fills it out and tells me where to sign. I thank her and walk across the street and hand the check to the *notaire*—and that's that. I own a house and car in France.

II

The Oil Guys

Mom returns to New York soon after the closing, and I stay at Chez Sally to work on the house—moving the furniture Monsieur and Madame Nedelec left, then putting it back where they had it; painting walls that are so damp I have to repaint them in the summer. I leave at the end of February, exhausted, happy, and fulfilled, and return in June ready to begin my life as a *propriétaire* on my own little pied-à-terre. I feel baronial on the flight to Paris and the trains to Brest and Loscoat, and it lasts all the way to the house, when I open the door and realize there's no one here but me, and I have to do everything, and there's nothing I know how to do, starting with the purchase of heating oil.

The water for the house—nine radiators, three sinks, bath-tub, and shower—is heated by a huge red rectangular box that looks like a fire engine standing upright. Turning the thing on scares the hell out of me. It sounds like a jet being ignited for take-off. Each time, I expect the worst, just as I do every time I fly: I know there will be a disaster, and each time it doesn't happen doesn't make me safer but brings me closer to the time it will. Each time I go into the stone shed, hold my breath, and push the start button I think: *This time.* The heater runs on oil that is housed in a 1,000-liter tank behind the shed. This is what's on my mind because Monsieur and Madame made it very clear I should never, *ever* allow the fuel to fall below a certain level (Or what? *What!*), and it was just above that level when I left in February. I find the fuel guy's business card among the cards Monsieur and Madame left for me. He's the same person they used. He knows the house, the heater, the tank, the whole routine—what's to worry? With confidence and two months of the Alliance Française, I pick up the phone and dial. "Bon-jour," I sing.

He answers, "Allo."

"Je suis l'American"—I'm the only one in the village—"le nouveau propriétaire chez Kostez Gwer."

"Oui."

That's it? *Oui.* Shit. He's waiting for *me* to say more. He's the fuel guy. Why else would I be calling? How am I supposed to know his office is in his home, as is nearly everyone else's, and no one pays for two phone lines, one for the business, one for home, so anyone could be calling for anything—and no one but a very good friend or an idiot would call during lunch? I finally manage to convey that I'm calling for *fuel* by repeatedly yelling, "Fuel, fuel, fuel," into the phone. It's my first business encounter on the phone, and I'm proud of myself. His English is good enough to say "Tomorrow." My French is good enough to understand "matin," morning. And sure enough, always a miracle to me and a crapshoot, he arrives the next morning in a huge tanker truck. I watch from the second-floor study window as a burly, balding, middle-aged man in spotless, pressed-with-a-crease, royal blue overalls slowly uncoils the hose and drags it, resisting as if it's alive and knows better, to the shed. Five minutes later he's knocking on my door.

That's fast, I think, but this is France, and what do I know? I open the door and he shakes my hand and immediately starts talking. He's calm, but I can see he's concerned. He doesn't begin with "Bonjour," so I know he's serious. What I don't know is what he is serious about. I nod, shrug, intermittently say, "Bon . . . Bon . . . Oui . . . Ah oui . . ." I know what he's telling me is important and I need to understand him, but I also know only a moron would be standing in his own doorway, in his house in France, discussing his heater with a French man, in French, and not speak the language. This is my first summer on my own, when I still think the worst thing I can be is a fool. I haven't yet realized that, given the circumstances, it's all I can be. But empirical knowledge is hard to deny, and day after year has confirmed it, so today I accept my basic fool-ness: Hi. I'm Mark, and I'm a fool. *Je suis un fou*—a truly humbling and humanizing experience for a middle-aged, moderately successful take-charge kind of guy. Type double-A American.

Meanwhile, I'm "bon, bonne-ing," and "ah oui-ing," trying to bluff my way through, preferring to have the house blow up than be a jerk. Finally, out of frustration or hopelessness or the desire to return to his life or his next appointment or lunch, he takes my hand and leads me like a three-year-old out the door, around the house, behind the shed. In the U.S., if this big, strong, bald man-of-a-man grabbed my hand, I would have hit him or run away. In France, I follow. He points at the tank, and says, "Voilà!"

"Oui," I say, like yes, that's the tank, or yes, that's where the oil goes, or yes sir, fill 'er up. He keeps chatting, louder and faster, and pointing. I keep nodding and saying, "Oui." He looks at me incredulously—in a way no one in the politically correct Bay Area would dare to—then leads me to the tank, kneels down, rubs his hand underneath it, and shows me the rust. Then he runs his finger across his neck and says, "Kaput," either figuring he'd have better luck with German or confirming German as the universal language for death. Either way, my tank is dead.

Through elaborate hand motions, along with spreading his arms, making bursting, exploding gestures and sounds, then stooping down and running all over the grass, he explains the tank will burst if he fills it, and a thousand liters of oil will cover everything. I get it: the tank has to be replaced. I point to him, full of hope and ask, "Vous?"

"Non."

"Qui?"

He shrugs, then takes me by the hand and leads me inside the shed. There, on the fire engine–red heater, is a sticker with the name of a business in a neighboring town.

"Oui?" I say.

He shrugs, shakes my hand, and leaves. "Bonne chance," he calls as he drives away, a free and happy man.

In the U.S., my next call would be to a lawyer. The people I bought the house from had lied. They knew about it and misled me. But even to me, the son of a lawyer, it's obvious that's not the case. Monsieur and Madame did everything, went above and beyond, waxed the floors and stairs, installed overhead lighting because I mentioned I preferred it, gave me a car, left me dishes, silverware, a bed, armoire, tables, chairs, cleaned the septic tank, none of which was called for or required, so why would they cheat me over an oil tank? Not only do I not call a lawyer—I don't call them. To this day, they do not know about the tank, because I know if they knew they'd feel bad, and I don't want them to feel that way at all. I don't want these people, my new friends, to think I'm a burden and they need to take care of me, watch over me, light candles, and make offerings to Saint Rita. So, with less confidence than before, I call the number on the sticker on the heater and open with the one sentence in French I think I say perfectly, "Parlez vous d'anglais?"

"Oui."

"Really?"

"Yes. A little."

Merde. I know what that means. I probably just heard ninety percent of his vocabulary. Still, there's nothing else for me to do but talk on. I explain about the oil guy, the tank, the kind of tank—metal—the size, location, and ask him if he does such work.

"Yes. Of course." Then he explains the work. First, it is necessary to drain the old tank and make sure it is clean and empty. Otherwise, when it is removed it will leak and create a mess. That's the hardest part. Very difficult. When it's done, a new tank must replace it.

"The price?"

"Twenty-five thousand francs." About $4,000.

"How long will it take?"

"One day."

"When can you do it?"

"Next week. Friday."

"Bon," I say, though $4,000 is a lot for me.

"Bon," he says, "Vendredi matin. Friday morning."

"Oui." Aside from being out $4,000 I hadn't expected to spend, I'm pretty happy. I did the whole deal by myself.

In the afternoon, I tell Madame P, and she goes nuts. She points her index finger to her temple and makes a rapid circular motion. "Pourquoi, pourquoi?" Why didn't I call her, she demands, and she tells me she knows a man—*un spécialiste, un artisan*—who would do the work better and for less, "moins cher, moins cher." She says the word "artisan" as if it is mythical and the phrase "moins cher" like a mantra, which I've come to learn it is, like *solde*, sale. I say I'm sorry—"Je suis désolé, je suis désolé," and I am, but it's over, done, "C'est fini." And to make sure she gets it, I explain it to her son Philippe, who's visiting from Cherbourg and fluent in English.

"A deal is a deal," I tell him. "I told the man 'Yes,' *in English*." I explain how everyone in France, Brittany, Finistère, Plobien has been straight with me, fair and honest, and I intend to be that way in return. Madame listens as Philippe translates what I said and goes nuts again. She starts to mock me, a side of her I haven't seen before. She rubs her index finger and thumb together in the universal gesture of money and calls me a fool—"fou, riche Américain, méchant," crazy, mad. My decision clearly offends her. It isn't until much later that I realize she feels responsible for me and that this decision and the way I'm responding tell her I need more help than even she suspected. I'm almost fifty years old and haven't taken a berating like this in forty years. I return home exhausted.

The following day, at noon, *midi*, when no self-respecting French person does anything except eat, there's a knock on my door. I open it, thinking it's Madame still on the warpath. Facing me is a short, bulky fellow in grease-stained blue worker's overalls, sweating profusely and wiping his nose. I don't know who he is, but I find his appearance assuring and unsettling: assuring because he looks like a *real* worker, unsettling because I've never seen a worker like him in France. All the French workers I've seen, no matter what their job, look like surgeons. He shakes my hand and immediately begins talking.

The only words I understand are "Madame P." I have no idea what she's done or said, but this guy is clearly here for something. I wait for him to finish and stand there frozen, mute. I haven't a clue. Then, like everyone else, he takes my hand and leads me out the door, around the house, behind the shed, to the oil tank. Ah, he's Madame's friend, *l'artisan*, who will do the work better and for less. I'm furious. She's cunning, sending him here at *midi*, when she knows I'll be home and don't have the vocabulary to send him away.

He removes a tape measure from his pocket and measures the door of the shed. He goes into the shed and measures some more. He comes out and measures the doorway again, as if while he was inside it magically changed its height or width. He measures everywhere and writes nothing down, so he has to measure it again. I watch him, amazed. He reminds me of one of the seven dwarfs, and I hope it isn't Dopey. I'm sure this is going to be a disaster.

He finally leaves, and as if on cue, Madame P arrives, all smiley and happy with her good deed, which lasts as long as it takes me to explain again that I've already agreed to let the other guy do it. And now, after having met Monsieur l'Artisan, I'm even more convinced my decision is right. But she isn't. She calls me "un riche Américain, un fou, méchant," and makes the crazy sign with her finger again, only this time spinning with both hands. Now what? If I don't choose her guy, she's going to be disappointed and hound me to death, maybe even leave me to fend for myself. If I *do* choose her guy, I'm going to break my word to the other guy, as well as the pledge I made to myself, and hire a guy who could be Dopey, and wind up having to pay the first guy to do all the work Dopey didn't do right.

Madame leaves, and Monsieur l'Artisan returns. Clearly, my life is a farce. He walks to the shed, measures everything again to be sure nothing's changed, and hands me a sheet of paper. I look at it. It's a *devis*, a binding estimate, an assumption I'm considering him for the work. I'm about to hand it back to him when I see the price, 3,000 francs, $500, which confirms (1) he's a crank and (2) his work is worthless—or (3) Madame is right. I now have a dilemma, which is becoming my common experience in France, pitting core belief against core belief. On one side, there's a deal, and I'm always searching for a deal, even though I'm always convinced whatever I pay, I paid too much. On the other side, you get what you pay for, and $500 is 12 percent of $4,000, which is about the result I expect. I don't know what to do, but he *is* Madame's friend, and it *is* a deal, so I halfheartedly, doubtfully, pursue it.

I lead him behind the stone shed where the old, rusty tank is and knock on it—it's metal, hard, durable—and point to the *devis*. "Le même?"

"Non."

Ha. I knew it.

"Supérieur." He takes me by the hand and leads me back inside the shed. "Ici." He points to a space next to the fire engine–red heater. "Plus facile."

I see. It's next to the heater, which makes it easier to connect, less copper tubing, fewer connections, easier, faster, cheaper. "Bon."

I knock on the heater and try my luck with "me-tal," which may or may not be a French word and may or may not mean metal.

"Non." He shakes his head. "Plastique." I knew it. Junk. Garbage. "C'est meilleur. Supérieur. C'est très bien pour l'intérieur. Pas de soleil, pas de rouille."

"Rouille?"

He takes me by the hand and leads me back outside to the tank. He bends down, swipes the bottom of the tank, and shows me a handful of rust. "Rouille."

I get it. Plastic won't rust. The problem with plastic is heat, the sun, and inside the shed it's protected, superior, *meilleur*. "C'est guarantee?"

"Oui. Bien sûr. Dix ans," and he shows me where it's written on the *devis*.

It sounds so good I'm convinced I'm going to get swindled. It's another of those conflicting beliefs: if it's too good to believe, it probably is—unless this is the time it isn't. I'm trying to figure how he's going to nail me. I knock on the tank again and point over the horizon, far, far away to another galaxy or my neighbor's yard, and say, "Au revoir, au revoir," while knocking on the tank and waving.

"Oui, oui," he says, not even blanching. "Au revoir."

"Combien plus?" It's the best French I have. "How much more?"

"Deux cents francs." Two hundred francs, about $35.

That's when I remember the oil, the dirty, rusty oil in the bottom of the tank that the first oil guy said was the real problem. Getting it out without cracking the tank and carrying it away without spilling. "Very difficult," he said, "lots of work," which in every language means more money.

I knock on the tank again and indicate its interior and say, "Huile," which is the word for cooking oil, not heating oil. "Ce n'est pas nettoyer." It's not clean, a phrase I learned from Kathryn at Chez Sally. "C'est difficile et cher—au revoir." It's hard and expensive to go bye-bye.

"No problème. J'ai une machine."

"Combien plus?"

"Deux cents francs." It seemed to be the answer for everything.

I now have a choice and a dilemma: $600 or $4,000; Madame's friend, Monsieur l'Artisan, or a guy who speaks English; to break my word and my pledge, or not.

The next two days Madame hounds me. Don't be a fool. Don't spend the money. She makes rich American money signs with her left hand and crazy signs with her right. Still, I don't relent. I gave my word and made the deal. That's that. She gets Philippe to call me and explain how I'm being taken, paying too much, how the artisan is a good man who does good work. I tell him, "I know, I know, but I gave my word. It's a contract."

"Ah," he says. "It's a matter of principle."

"Oui."

"I see. Yes. I will tell my mother." He hangs up.

Once again, I see there's a code. Had I said, "C'est le principe," all would have been accepted. Bon. Another lesson learned. The phone rings. It's Philippe. "Did you sign a paper?"

"No."

"Ah bon. In France, if you don't sign a paper you have seven days to change your mind."

I don't know if he's fooling me or not, if he made it up or his mother is making him say it. "Really?"

"Yes."

"C'est normal? Not a special gimmick for Americans?"

"Oui. Bien sûr."

I ask everyone I know, even people I don't know well, and they all say, yes, it is true, I have seven days to change my mind. So now I have another dilemma. I can change my mind, save $3,500, and not break my word or my pledge—but if I do, I have to work with Monsieur l'Artisan, about whom I still have my doubts.

On the sixth day, I decide to do it. I tell Madame, who looks as happy as Patton in Rome. She then offers to call the fellow and explain it to him in French, but this is my doing and I don't want her to do something I know French people are not comfortable doing, disappointing others, telling them no. So I call and explain how a friend of mine has a friend who has a tank and can install it this weekend, and I thank him for his help. He's fine with it—"No problem"—and offers his assistance, sounding as if he knows I'll need it.

I'm feeling pretty good, confident even, until the next day when Monsieur l'Artisan arrives pulling an open trailer carrying a 1,000-liter tank that has as much chance of fitting through the doorway of the shed as the proverbial camel through the eye of a needle. His son, a younger, not much smaller version of himself, hops out of the truck, and together they remove the tank and carry it to the shed. It's like watching a World Wide Wrestling father-and-son tag team in slow motion. The son scratches his head. Monsieur l'Artisan scratches his and shrugs. They talk back and forth for a few minutes, using lots of "ouis" and "nons." Then they go to work. Monsieur lifts the shed door from its hinges and lays it on the grass. His son removes the hinges from the door frame, while Monsieur unscrews all the attachments on the tank. All the while they're working, they're smoking. They're also sweating, because it's one of those magnificent hot—mid-eighties—navy blue cloudless days in Finistère.

I go into the house and return with two tall glasses of cold water. They each take one, thank me profusely, and put it down without taking a sip. I don't get it. Don't they trust me? Are they waiting for it to warm up? Do they want gin? Monsieur l'Artisan says something to his son, who says something back. Then, in unison, they stand the tank on its end and turn it, twist it actually, and thread it and screw it through the doorway, setting it in the place Monsieur had measured fifteen times to make sure it would fit. It was magic, sleight of hand at its best. When it's in place next to the red heater, they drink the water as if it's a prize or reward, thank me again, and return to work. I watch as they measure everything again, bang and cut and bend copper pipe, connecting the heater to the tank.

I go back to the house and wait, wondering how long it will take them. After two hours, I see them carrying their tools to the truck. I watch, suspicious, sure I'm about to be ripped off, even though they're doing all the work and I haven't yet paid them a sou. Still, when Monsieur l'Artisan gets behind the wheel and his son hops in the cab, I can't contain my American self. I run down the stairs calling, "Monsieur, Monsieur," to stop them.

Monsieur opens the window and looks at me. "Oui."

"Le tank." I point. "Le ancien tank," hoping tank means tank and not a fighting machine with tread.

"Oui, oui," he says. "Demain."

Tomorrow, right! I knew this would happen, that something would go wrong, and I'd have to pay the first guy to do the hardest, most expensive part of the job. I want to call Madame P, but I don't. I feel bad. There's no reason to make her feel worse. In the U.S. I would, but not here. She tried to help me and it didn't work out. Live with it. Lesson learned, though I'm not sure what it is.

Late the next day, when I've given up all hope, I hear a rattling commotion, jiggling, banging, a backfire, and look out the window. There, in my driveway—how it got in I'll never know—is a vehicle that looks part Oscar Meyer wienermobile, part Rube Goldberg, with more hoses and nozzles on it than a fire truck. Holy Christ, what is this?

I run out of the house to get it out of my yard when I see Monsieur l'Artisan emerge alone from the vehicle. He's beaming, proud as a first-time papa, petting his machine, stroking it like a lover. The thing's making noises like it could explode. He takes out a cigarette and lights it. I look around, getting ready to duck and cover. "Qu'est-ce que c'est?" I finally manage to sputter.

He hands me a brochure. It's in French. I try to read it—but he only has one life and can't wait for me to finish—so he proceeds to tell me and show me in great detail what this machine does. He pulls a hose from the wiener part of the vehicle, drags it across the lawn to the *ancien* rusty tank behind the shed, and connects it. He then explains through hand motions and disgusting slurping sounds how the machine will suck all the old, bad, dirty oil out of the tank so he can safely move it. Pretty good, I think, an oil vacuum. "Bon."

He takes me by the hand and leads me back to the vehicle and begins making washing motions and rolling his hands over each other like turning drums. I don't get it. He takes me to the rear of the thing, leading me along the hose, and starts making that disgusting sucking sound, like the oil being sucked away, then makes the rolling motion with his hands, and leads me to another nozzle and another hose, which he pulls out and connects to the new tank.

"Non?" I say.

"Oui," he says.

"Vous êtes faîtes?"

"Oui."

It's incredible. It really is. This guy living in rural Brittany, selling heating oil, invented a machine that not only removes old, rusty, filthy oil from broken tanks, thereby avoiding spillage, destruction, and waste, but it cleans and recycles the oil so it doesn't have to be dumped and can be used again, saving time, money, and nonrenewable energy. He's a genius. Who's Dopey now?

After him—Monsieur l'Artisan l'Inventeur—I never doubt Madame P again. I still have that plastic tank—guaranteed for ten years—and his son regularly fills it. When he sees it I'm sure he thinks nothing of it, just another job finished and done. But each time I go into the shed I remember that day and their work and Monsieur l'Artisan standing in my driveway patting his machine, proud as he could be, showing l'Américain his invention.

When his son comes to fill the tank or clean the heater or chimneys I always offer him a drink of juice, water, coffee, or tea, which he always refuses, telling me "later"—"après, après." When he's finished working he knocks on the door. I invite him in and we sit at the kitchen table and drink, him chatting away like his father, looking more and more like him, me understanding a third of what he says, both of us, at least for the moment, fulfilled and content.

This is what I love about France, the small things are large, a *bonjour, ça va*, a flower, a glass of water. It's a good way to live, and daunting—even more so I imagine for the French, who know the rules and what's expected of them and who are more worried about failing than I am. So we carry on, me and the oil guy and his son and everyone else I know by doing our best not to *faux pas*. . . . It *is* a good way to live.

The Floor Guy

One day I decide I need to have the wood floors in the house professionally cleaned, waxed, and protected. In the U.S. I would never think of such a thing, perhaps because I'm a renter, and this is what owning property does, but I think it has more to do with France herself.

In the U.S., I never notice dirt or dust or decay, only disorder. In the U.S., I organize. In France, I clean. I mop the floors. I get on my knees and wax the tile. I vacuum. In the U.S., I don't even own a vacuum cleaner. I bought a mop once, though I never remember where it is. I have a broom because it came with the apartment. Once a month a cleaning person comes and brings everything she needs, and that's that. In France, I'm the cleaning person. I've bought three vacuums, each stronger, more durable, with greater suck than the last, and now own a top-of-the-line Miele and am *proud* of it! And the pity of it is, it matters. I think it has to do with the French emphasis on cleanliness and appearance and my not wanting to be a blight on the country, taken for a Brit, or to offend or disappoint those who have done so much for me. I acknowledge them by cleaning, so that if at any time someone from the village or the water company or a neighbor stops by, Madame P and Monsieur and Madame Nedelec will not be shunned or accused of bringing a derelict or neo-Brit into town. It's France: I clean, therefore I am. I even do windows.

And like everyone else, I have a special product for everything. I have a sponge mop, a cloth mop, and a rag mop; a mop for dusting wood, washing tile, clearing spiderwebs; brooms for indoors, outdoors, wood, tile, walls; and cleaning supplies for anything: kitchen sink, bathroom sink, tub, shower, windows, wood, tile, plaster, stove, fabric, stone, toilets, toilet smells, burners, microwave, dishwasher, kitchen smells, and the all-purpose mystery cleaner, Javel, which if used unmasked in a closed room for more than thirty seconds will kill you. Masked, with all the windows open, I'm good for five minutes. After that I'm woozy.

One afternoon while drinking coffee with Sharon, I ask her, more out of curiosity than interest, "What are those tiny piles of sawdust on the floor?" She looks and says "Woodworm," something I never even knew existed. The piles are so small and infrequent and without any pattern or apparent threat and the floors are so thick I decide, Who cares.

So it is a great surprise to me when I wake up a few days later thinking about the floors and the woodworms. My first reaction is to ignore the thought and go to the beach, which I do. But every day after that the floors never look the same. After a week of this, I decide to do something if it's not too expensive. I do what I always do when I decide to do something in France: I call Madame P and ask if she knows a floor guy. "Connait vous un person nettoye plancher?" Know you a person clean floor? It's the kind of question that makes her day. First, it confirms my basic humanity and intelligence, and the fact that I'm not English, and second, it sets her into action.

As with all things like this, once I set the ball rolling I never know what will happen next, or when. If it's an emergency, like a doctor or food, the response is immediate. If it's like this—floors—it could take weeks, during which time I usually give up or forget I even asked. This is one of those times that takes weeks.

It's late afternoon and I'm napping. I hear a pounding on the door that scares the bejesus out of me. Either the person has been knocking for quite some time and has grown frustrated or worried, or it's the end of the world.

"*Moment*," I yell, and run down the stairs to see who it is. In the U.S., I'd ignore the knocking or demand an ID before opening the door. I yank open the door, which sticks in the rain, and see the biggest French person I've ever seen. Not big fat. Big like a bear. Huge. Jean-Paul Bunyan, with a chest like a cask, arms like giant legs of lamb, and he's beaming, smiling like a toothpaste commercial, which is odd because usually strangers look wary, doubtful, or scared when they meet me.

"Bonjour," he bellows, clearly happy to be here. He's either lost, a loon, on drugs, or the happiest guy in France. He's wearing spotless, white, pressed worker's overalls. I have no idea who he is or what he wants. He shakes my hand, hands me a card, and says something about Henri, Madame P's younger son. The card is in French and English—Proper Plancher—so I start speaking in English until I realize his English is worse than my French.

I invite him in, pointing to the kitchen, but he does what most French people do when I speak, he ignores me. He takes two steps forward, kicks off his shoes, gets down on all fours, crawls to the stairs, and begins knocking on the first step, stroking it softly and smelling it. He works his way up three stairs, then knocks and rubs his way down and turns left into the library–game room, where he crawls around some more, knocking everywhere and mumbling to himself all the way. I figure the house is about to collapse or it's a shrine, an oil well, a gold mine. I can't tell—only that this guy, Hugo!— what kind of French name is that?—is thunderstruck. I watch in awe as this bear of a man crawls around my floor "bon-ing" and "oui-ing" and rubbing. Even I know this isn't usual first-time-meeting-someone behavior.

I finally get him into the kitchen, which has a tile floor, so I think I'm safe, but he immediately begins "bon-ing" and "oui-ing" as he caresses the wood paneling covering the old stone kitchen fireplace. I can't tell if he's going to have an orgasm, a heart attack, or both. Finally he sits down and tells me the floors are original, more than 100 years old, very rare. He shows me the thickness and width of the planks and tells me, to my relief, that they are in excellent condition and that he hasn't seen anything this old in this good condition in years. I'm nodding, happy, thrilled, still not sure if this guy's a lunatic or for real, thinking he's trying to sell me some polish or wax or service I don't need.

He must sense my skepticism because he leaves the table and goes to his van and returns with two photo albums, each at least eight inches thick. I'm hoping like hell it's not what he did last summer. He opens the first book and shows me pictures of magnificent floors before, during, and after he's worked on them, house after house after house, châteaux, the Beaux Arts museum in Quimper. No doubt about it, if this album and work are his, this guy's for real.

I walk him through the rest of the house so he can see it. In every room, including the attic, he hits the floor and crawls around "bon-ing" and "oui-ing," knocking and rubbing, saying, "Magnifique, original, beau, ancien," and makes that inhaling whistling noise that sounds to me like incoming.

After about thirty minutes we're back at the kitchen table. Casually, as if being polite but not really interested—I don't want him to get his hopes too high—I ask him for an estimate, *un devis*. He shakes his head and tells me he's very busy and not sure he can do the job. Now I really want him, and I'm ready to pay almost anything. Thinking of the photos in the album, I'm willing to beg. With floors like this, Madame P and Monsieur and Madame Nedelec would be proud of me. That's when he tells me about his son, Johann—another odd French name—and the trip they took to New York, which both of them loved and because of that trip and I'm American, yes, he will do the job. He says he'll send me the *devis* by mail. He also says his friend will come to the house and give me a *devis* for *le traitement*.

I'm perplexed. "Quel traitement?" In the U.S. it would be included—varnish, wax, whatever.

He takes me by the hand and leads me into the library-game room and points at a tiny pile of sawdust on the floor. Ah, for the woodworm. "Bon."

It's early June. The work is to be done in September or October, after his mandatory August vacation and before my November rental arrives. We shake hands, and that's that.

By mid-July there's still no *devis*, and Monsieur le Traitement has yet to arrive. If August arrives before the floor guy and his *traitement* buddy, it's over for this year, and suddenly, though I never in my life cared about it before, I want my floors done now. It used to be Peace Now, End the War Now, Bring the Troops Home Now, and now it's Finish My Floors by November, please. Once again, I learn Marx was right.

My first instinct is to call Monsieur and Madame P and scream, "*Attention!*" but I know better. If I call, they'll feel responsible for the work, the price, and the outcome, and it will make them even more nervous and anxious than they are. French people are often nervous and anxious. They're fatalists, certain that whatever they do, it won't work out. That's why the theater of the absurd. That's why "C'est la vie." Shit happens. Americans say it, but truly don't expect it and are outraged and dismayed when it does. The French do not say it, but they await its downpour every day. I decide to spare Monsieur and Madame an additional load and resort to guerrilla tactics. I do the one thing I know will drive the floor guy nuts. I make it an issue of national pride.

"Bonjour. C'est Monsieur Greenside, l'Américain. Où est le *devis*? Au revoir." I do this to let people know I'm not a Brit, and because contrary to international myth, most French people like Americans—not the government or much of the culture but the people—and there's an unspoken rivalry and competition between the countries, much like the Giants and Dodgers. When I say I'm American, the French usually rise to the challenge.

The next day there's a knock on the door. I run down the stairs, triumphant, certain I've prevailed where Peter Mayle had not. I open the door, trying not to gloat, expecting to see the floor guy, *devis* in hand, maybe looking bashful. Ha.

Facing me is a tall, thin, fair, very curly-haired lad wearing wire-rim glasses. He's dressed casually in tan chinolike pants and a cucumber green dress shirt. He looks like an intellectual or a salesman selling the Great Books or encyclopedias. "Hello," he says, holding out his hand, "I'm Johann."

The floor guy's son. I shake his hand and say "Bonjour," emboldened by his English.

"I am here to measure the floors."

"Good, good. Come in." I'm thrilled he's here and thrilled he speaks English. I follow him around the house as he measures each floor and writes down the numbers. He's a student, premed, studying in the south of France. In the summers, he works for his dad. He wants to talk about New York, California, the U.S., books, literature, why I'm there, if I like it, what I write—he's heard I'm a writer—and he wants to practice his English. I, of course, want to practice my French. We have a very long, odd conversation made up of words that don't exist in either language, until *midi*—noon, lunchtime—when he leaves, promising the *devis* the next day.

Sure enough, about the same time the next day, there's knocking on my door. I run down the stairs, pull open the door, and say "Johann," as I thrust out my hand to shake.

In front of me is an openmouthed middle-aged guy whose name apparently is not Johann. He shakes my hand and steps backward, not an easy thing to do, and says something I don't understand, so I shrug and say "Oui." He removes a card from his clipboard and hands it to me. The only things I can read are his name and the word *traitement*. Ah, Monsieur le Traitement!

"Entrée," I say, "entrée." I say it as if I just won the lottery.

He hesitates, clearly not accustomed to this kind of enthusiasm. I point to the floor in the library–game room and say, "S'il vous plaît," which spurs him to action. He removes a tape measure from his belt and measures the floor from north to south, south to north, east to west, and west to east, as well as diagonally. He does this in every room, working fast, faster than I've ever seen a French worker work. Either he has other important plans or he wants out of here and away from me very badly. He's done in twenty minutes. I expect him to do what every other French worker has done—shake my hand and tell me the *devis* will be in the mail. He sits at the kitchen table and begins writing and figuring, crossing out numbers, replacing them with others, checking everything with his calculator. He finally finishes and hands me the paper—I'm expecting the worst. I look at the bottom line, which is all I can read anyhow: 5,500 francs, about $1,000. Guaranteed for ten years. He tells me this by saying "Garanti" and holding up ten fingers.

I'm amazed. "Pas de insecte pour dix année?"

"Oui."

"Vous êtes guarantee?"

"Oui."

"Vous êtes écrit le guarantee?"

"Oui." He's beginning to look at me oddly.

"Combien?"

He points to the number on the *devis*, clearly wondering if I'm compos mentis and authorized to make this deal.

"No, no. Maintenant. En avance. Avant."

"Zéro."

"Zero?"

"Zéro."

"Bon." I shake his hand.

He hands me a pen, shows me where to sign, and I do. Then he gives me a copy and shakes my hand again, and that is that. I now have a deal with a man I've never met before to kill worms I've never seen, for a thousand dollars, to be paid at some indefinite time in the future, *after* the work is done. In the U.S., my own sister wouldn't do business with me this way.

I'm starting to feel pretty optimistic. I might actually have the floors done this year. Three weeks later, a week before I'm due to leave, I still don't have the floor guy's *devis*. I telephone again and get the floor guy's secretary, who I find out later is his wife. I explain I'm the American and I'm leaving in a week and I still don't have the *devis*.

"Demain," she says. Tomorrow.

All day I wait, resist calling, telling myself to give him until five o'clock. In the U.S., I'd be furious and telephoning every fifteen minutes. In France, I wait, not because I want to, but because there's nothing else I can do. Who would I complain to, the U.S. embassy? At six o'clock, there's a loud knocking. I look out the window and see it's the floor guy— Hugo—holding a clipboard. *"Moment,"* I yell, and run down the stairs to the door. I open it and hold out my hand. He grabs me and hugs me like a California guy. He's beaming, waving his clipboard, and talking away. I shrug several times, say "Oui . . . Oui . . . Ah, oui," hoping I haven't just given him the house or the right to raise pigs in my yard.

"Entrée," I say, pointing to the kitchen so he can give me the *devis* to sign. He goes into the library–game room and begins measuring, north to south, south to north. . . . I explain Johann has already measured every room and so has Monsieur le Traitement. "Oui, oui," he says, and keeps measuring, writing the numbers down on his pad. He measures every floor, as if somehow the numbers could have changed. In the U.S., I'd be offended, as if the guy is accusing me of trying to cheat him, like I sneaked in a few extra feet of floor I'm trying to get worked on for free. In France, I recognize it for what it is: precision, personal responsibility, and not believing anyone else could do it as accurately as he. I know the routine, so I wait for him at the kitchen table. When he finishes he sits at the table and begins figuring, adding, multiplying, then adding some more. I'm getting scared. I'm in way over my head. What the hell was I thinking? I need floors done like I need root canal. He shows me the number—30,000 francs, almost $6,000—not a lot for the work, but a lot for me. I've already said yes for the $1,000 *traitement*. With this, it's $7,000 total, and knowing what I know about workers and work and old houses, I suspect it will be even more. I'm not going to embarrass him by offering him less, and I don't have the money to say yes. I'm stymied.

That's when he starts talking about Johann. He tells me again about their trip to New York and how much they liked the city. He tells me about Johann's studies and what a good boy he is, how hard he works, how smart, and he asks me about his English. Is it good? Does he understand? Does he speak well? Did I like him when he came to the house? I'm yes-ing him all over the place, "Oui. Oui, Oui." He's so proud of his son.

The more I "oui'"d, the more he went on. Johann loves English. He's studying English, reads it all the time, wants to know more. "Oui, oui, c'est bon." He wants to go back to the United States, to Florida, New Orleans, California. "Oui, oui, oui. C'est joli." I'm thrilled. I'm following the conversation, I understand, I'm responding correctly. I have no idea why he is telling me all this, but it's great. We're talking, communicating, being friendly. He asks if Johann could come to the house and speak English with me. And if Johann ever came to the U.S., could he call me if he has a problem or needs help? Could he stay with me if he visits San Francisco? "Oui, oui, bien sûr." Being very strange in a strange land, I understood completely. I like Johann and I like this guy, his enthusiasm for everything, and his obvious pride in his son.

"Bon," he finally says, and stands.

The *devis* is on the table between us. He picks it up, folds it in quarters, and puts it in one of his many pockets. I have no idea what this means. I don't think I've offended him. He doesn't seem angry. He's smiling, shakes my hand, and gives me another of those California manly bear hugs, and leaves. All I can figure is he doesn't want the work, it's not worth it to him, or he's sensed I don't have the money and he's protecting both of us from my embarrassment.

Three days later, the day before I'm leaving for California, there's a knock on the door. I run down the stairs and open the door. It's Hugo holding his clipboard. I put out my hand to shake. He pulls me toward him and I brace myself for another backbreaking hug.

"Entrée," I say. No matter how many times people have been to the house, including Madame P, who visits almost daily, no one will enter unless I say "Entrée." No one will sit unless I say "Asseyez vous." And when I offer a drink of juice, beer, wine, water, no one will pour it for him- or herself or begin drinking until I sit down and pour it for them. Nothing is taken for granted. So, beaming and bear hug aside, I'm wondering why he's here—but this is France, so the last thing I'll do is ask. We talk about New York, Johann, English, visiting the United States, the weather, my trip back to California, his wife, Nadine, who is a wonderful cook, and he invites me to his house for *poisson* next summer when I return.

I still don't have a clue what's happening, and I don't until he removes a piece of paper from his clipboard and hands it to me. The *devis*. Shit, I think, I've been snookered. He's softened me up for the kill. These people are wily, I think, all friendly and then wham-bang. I look at the bottom line and see he's given me an incredible bargain. Ashamed, I look at him, wanting to say something, but all I can manage is, "Merci, merci. C'est bien?"

"Bon," he says, smiling.

I sign it and ask how much is the down payment?

"Rien."

"Rien?"

"Rien."

"Bon." And that's it. I give him a key to the house—one of at least a dozen available in the village—and leave the next day, not sure what will await me when I return.

By the end of October the work is complete, as agreed. Everyone, including the November renters, tells me the floors and stairs are beautiful. They are several shades lighter, making the whole house brighter, and I'm anxious to pay the bill. Money is strange in France. Outwardly, people disdain it—even shopkeepers—but they remember every sou. I don't want money to come between us. I send him a Christmas card and ask for the bill. Nothing. June arrives, I'm ready to return, and I still don't have the bill eight months after he's completed the work. I figure he must have left it in the house, but when I arrive it's not there. Clearly, I'm more concerned about this than he is.

A few weeks later, I see his van in the village: green and white, with *Proper Plancher* written on it. I walk toward it, overwhelmed by the pungent smell of glue, wax, and varnish. It's like a Dickens factory of the 1800s. My head's woozy

even though I'm standing meters away. This odor makes
Javel smell like an air freshener. I walk up to the van with my
eyes watering, gulping air. Hugo is sitting inside talking on
his mobile phone. I stand there waiting for him to finish his
conversation. My head's wobbly. I'm afraid my nose is going
to start to bleed, my ears ooze, I'm going to faint from the
fumes. French workers don't wear goggles, masks, earplugs.
No protection—they rarely wear helmets on motorcycles.
He's sitting there laughing and chatting away, then abruptly
closes the phone, clearly upset, and says, "Merde." He stares
at the phone, shakes it, and waves it in front of me. I can barely
stand, see, breathe. I feel nauseated. "This thing is killing
me," he says, "X-rays, gamma, micro—le cancer," he's yelling, more worried about the phone than he is about sitting in
his van, which smells like the Cuyahoga River on a bad day.
I back away, staggering. Maybe this is why he's the happiest
man I've met in France. It's either that or his wife's *poisson*,
which I eat later that summer and is as every bit as wonderful
as he said, cooked with herbs, veggies, and spices fresh from
her garden.

I pay Hugo in July, and in December the floods come—
l'inondation—and for the first time in anyone's memory my
house floods. I knew the river overflowed when I bought
the house. Madame P told me her house had flooded several
times in recent years, but my house was supposed to be safe.
It's farther back from the river. The floodplain is uphill and
large. Water should not have been able to reach my house. I
find out later what happened. The river is dammed, and the
dam was under great pressure from huge amounts of rain and
high tides, so they opened the dam to release the pressure and
flooded the villages below. Madame P has water, mud, and a
couple of salmon floating in three feet of water in her kitchen

and dining room. I have two inches on my ground floor. The front hallway, kitchen, and medieval garden-party room have tile floors and are ok. The library–game room, newly refinished by Hugo, is ruined, warped and buckled by the water.

I just paid him for the original work and now I need more. The good news is it should be covered by my insurance. The bad news is, I have to see my insurance guy to get it.

The Insurance Guy

A few days after closing on the house and signing documents I couldn't read or understand, I went to an insurance agent, where I signed several more documents I couldn't read or understand. The insurance man was in his mid-sixties, well dressed in tie and tweeds, very flush in the face, and looked familiar. I realized while sitting there and signing documents that he was one of the old guys I saw in the bar every day with his glass of red at seven in the morning when I got my daily bread. I don't know if this is good news or not, whether it will make it easier to make a claim or harder. He's jovial and pleasant, and I expect, as in the U.S., I'll never see him again, and I don't.

He retires shortly afterward and passes the business on to his son, a lovely young man whose worst nightmare is me. Every professional has one. It's the client you do the most for: you help, advise, direct, lead by the hand, bend the rules, feed if necessary, hold, do more for and charge less, expect less, make compromises you never thought you'd make and never made before—all for no apparent or tangible reason, none of which the client sees, appreciates, understands, recognizes, or acknowledges. You tell the person the same thing over and over and over again, and he never does what you say. At some point in the all too near future, you know two things for sure: (1) you're going to have to tell the person everything again; and (2) he's not going to do what you told him, there's going to be a problem, and you're the only one who can fix it.

That's me with the insurance guy. I want to understand. I want to do what he tells me, but he speaks so fast—mostly, I think, to get me out of his office—that I understand nothing. So I return a few days later and ask the same question and drive him nuts. This has become our routine. I do everything I can to help him, and he does everything he can to help me, and more often than not, we fail. It's pitiful.

I know I could ask Madame or Monsieur Nedelec or one of my other bilingual friends to come with me, but French people have such a natural aversion, fear, and loathing of anything bureaucratic or official, I don't want to ask. People break out in hives, twitch, get sick if they have to deal with the bureaucracy, which makes life difficult because there is so much of it. Mail is okay, probably because the person delivering it is local and it's face-to-face, but the telephone is a problem.

The French don't like the telephone—they like to see the person they're dealing with, the expression, mood, and body language, so they know how to react—except, of course, if they're talking with a bureaucrat, whom they don't want to see at all. Ever. And bureaucrats feel the same way. They don't want to see their clients. The system works fine, based on mutual distrust and loathing: bureaucrat does job, never sees client; client gets service, never sees bureaucrat. Professional distance, distance between client and worker, is great, and actual contact kept to a minimum. (No wonder therapy hasn't caught on in Brittany. The last thing you'd want to tell your therapist is anything personal.) Everyone likes it this way, except me. I'm middle-aged, Jewish, the son of a lawyer, I read the *San Francisco Chronicle*, listen to talk radio, and watch local Fox news: thinking up disasters comes naturally. I wake up with nightmare questions about my house. What happens if . . . ? and I want to talk to my agent. That's when the problems begin.

For example, I've asked all my French friends what happens if I've been drinking and have a serious car accident and wipe out a herd of cows. Could I lose my house? Everyone looks at me aghast. The first time I asked I felt like a pedophile asking them where the kids are. I learn—after many responses—that it isn't the situation that frightens them, that I'd actually do it or contemplate doing it or that they've driven with me and didn't know I had these instincts or proclivities. No, what scares them is (1) I could even think of it, and (2) it's possible—even likely—in the U.S.

"No," they all say. "Here, in France, it's not possible."

I'm reassured, but I want to hear it from my insurance agent. I don't know why this is such an obsessive question, but it is. Maybe it has to do with how much money I've put into the house. Given the way the French drive—and the way I drive in France—hitting a herd of cows is certainly a possibility. So if losing the house is likely, why spend extra money on it? Like why fix the gate if I'm going to lose the house in some French trickster insurance scam? That's what I want to know from my agent.

I never make an appointment to see him. To my way of

thinking it's more informal and less threatening if I just stop by. To his way of thinking he's caught, dead, trapped, cornered. At this point in our relationship (in all my relationships in France) I know I should call (French people don't like to be surprised), but if I do, he's going to ask me what it's about and I won't be able to explain on the phone. All I'll be able to say is "L'assurance," which isn't going to help him a lot. If I make an appointment—say, *mardi à quinze heures*, Tuesday at three in the afternoon—he'll worry from the time of the call to the meeting about what I'm going to ask, need, say, and how he's going to fail me again. This is what bothers him most, what bothers most French people, not knowing (which is why they don't like surprises), not succeeding, not being able to help, failing. He tries so hard, I feel sorry for him, so I don't call. Why ruin two days for him when I can just drop by his office and ruin an hour?

As soon as I walk in he stands, shakes my hand, offers me a seat, a pen, calendar, anything, trying to anticipate or imagine what it is I'm here for and hoping it's over soon.

I sit down, then he sits down. He holds his hands together in front of him, fingers folded together in a prayerful way, forcing himself to be calm.

"Bonjour," I say. "J'ai une question."

"Ouuuui," he says, squinting.

He's reacting the same way I do whenever a girlfriend says, "We have to talk." I ignore him the way they ignore me and go on. "Par example. Je conduit le voiture et beaucoup la vache sur la route—et voilà! Bang!—beaucoup morte vache. Si possible le propriétaire apprendre mon maison?" I finish, amazed actually that I got it out, but my amazement is nothing compared to his. He's dumbstruck, something virtually unheard of in France.

"Vous êtes compris?"

"Oui."

"C'est possible?"

He stands and goes to his files to get my file. It's like watching inertia made visible. It's not that he's slow, it's that it's hopeless and he knows it and whatever he says or does won't work and I'll feel bad and he'll feel worse.

He places my file on his desk, reads it over or pretends to because nobody whose left eye is blinking the way his is could read anything. He then points to a section of the agreement I signed and initialed, reads it out loud, and says, "Bon."

"Bon?"

"Oui."

"Oui, mais, par example, c'est possible je perdue la maison?"

All he wants is to get out of here, but it's three o'clock in the afternoon and we both know he's there till seven. He pretends to read further into the contract. "Normalement," he says, keeping his eyes on the page, and I know I'm in trouble. No eye contact means bad news and *normalement*, like *en principe*, means this is the way things are supposed to be, *and* they never are. He says a few more things I don't understand and concludes grimly and firmly with, "Normalement."

He just gave me a series of exceptions for when I could lose the house, and I don't understand any of them, which leaves me where I was when I started, ignorant, but he, my insurance agent, is shattered. Once again he's tried to help me and failed.

I thank him, stand, and shake his hand. His smile is forced and both of his eyes are now blinking. I feel awful. I want to help him, empower him, give him a chance to succeed. In the

U.S., communication is often competitive—I win, you lose, fuck you. But in France, I've learned, communication is about mutual success: If you succeed, I succeed, and I want to succeed very much. Using my best teaching voice and technique, I say, "Monsieur, j'ai un autre question."

He sinks to his chair with an audible sigh.

"Sur la maison."

He closes my car file, puts it back where he got it, and returns with my house file.

"Oui."

"J'ai une chambre plus."

"Oui." His eyes widen. The blinking stops. He shrugs. My rates will go up, I know it. Still, I've promised myself that I will be completely forthright, honest, and forthcoming in my dealings with people here, and I have something to tell him.

"Oui, le attic . . ." He looks blank. No recognition. It's a look I've seen before. One-third of all English words are French in origin, so I've got a one in three chance of getting it right by just changing the accent. "A-*tick*," I try; "*at*-ick." Still no recognition. Now I have to resort to acting. I hold my hand over my head. "La chambre en haute la maison est nouveau."

"Oui."

He says it the way I do when I haven't a clue.

"S'il vous plaît," I say, reaching for a piece of paper and a pen. I draw a picture of a house with an arrow pointing to the attic. "C'est nouvelle." I point, using *nouveau* and *nouvelle* interchangeably because I don't know the difference and hope one of them is right. "Beaucoup travaillé. Fine maintenant. Nouvelle chambre."

"Oui."

He says it like he's dealing with a three-year-old, which, given my language skills, is giving me a year or two. I plunge forward. "C'est nécessaire je payee plus d'assurance?" It's a question I would never in my life ask in the U.S.

He looks at me the way I feel. Only a nut would ask me this. Still, I've begun, so I persist. "Plus d'assurance, c'est nécessaire?" Maybe it's better backward.

He takes the pen from my hand, turns the paper over, and draws a house.

"Oui," I say.

He looks at me like, "Oui" what? but he knows it's useless. He draws an identical house next to the one I drew. Beneath the first house he writes "avant." Beneath the second he writes "après."

"Bon," I say. "Oui." Before and after. I get it.

"C'est la même," he says. "C'est la même." After repeating it twenty or thirty times, I finally do get it. The house is the same size, same number of square meters: nothing new has been added in space. I've been honest and forthright and forthcoming, and it hasn't cost me a franc. But I want to be sure, so I ask, "Ce n'est pas nécessaire payee plus d'assurance?"

"Non."

"Bon."

"Bon."

I'm thrilled, and the insurance guy is even more so. I'm finally leaving his office *and* I understand. He's happy and I'm happy—a mutual success.

Still, when the river overflows and the house floods and I have to make a claim, I'm not too sure. The last time I had a question, this time a claim. The last time it was my money I was asking about, this time it's his.

The good news is most of the furniture is saved thanks to Sharon and Jean, Martin and Louise (an English couple who recently moved to Plobien), and Madame P, who move things to higher ground before anything gets seriously soaked. The bad news is the rugs—old kilims—and all the furniture legs are damaged, and the newly redone floor in the library–game room is ruined. I have bills for the hours it took to clean the house of mud, silt, and salt stains, the cost of cleaning the rugs, and repairing the furniture. What I still need is an estimate from Hugo, the floor guy, to submit to the insurance guy so I can make my claim.

I call his office and get his wife, Nadine, again, and say "Bonjour" and "Ça va," and remind her who I am in case she forgot—"Je suis le Américaine dans Kostez Gwer"—I'm the American girl inside Kostez Gwer. "C'est nécessaire Monsieur visite moi pour l'inondation." It's necessary Monsieur visits me for the flood.

"Oui. Bien sûr," and she tells me tomorrow at three, "quinze heures," and invites me to their house for *poisson*.

The next day, at 3:15, there's a knock on the door. I'm amazed. I race down the stairs, open the door, and see Johann. I invite him in and we spend the afternoon chatting about American literature, the U.S., France, the world. When he leaves he tells me his father will be here next week.

"Quand?" I ask. "Quel jour?"

"La semaine prochaine." He shakes my hand.

A week later Hugo arrives. We begin by talking about Johann, his English, his future, a visit to the U.S., and he invites me to his house for dinner the following week. As far as I can see, nothing's changed: he's still the happiest man I know.

He sets about measuring the room as if he and his son and Monsieur Le Traitement have never measured it before and this is the first time he's been here. When he finishes, he tells me the floor is ruined, which I already know, and suggests replacing the old pine planks with chestnut. He tells me this by showing me the French word for chestnut—*châtaignier*—in the dictionary. He also suggests doing something under the floor, but I don't get it. After his fifth attempt to explain it to me, he walks to the farthest corner of the room, bends over, and rips a huge chunk of pine out of the floor. Holy shit! A minute ago I had a warped, ruined floor I could walk on. Now I have a warped, ruined floor with a one-foot by two-foot hole in it that's pouring cold, winter air into the house.

"Bon," he says, and points to the hole, indicating he wants me to look in. I look and see the floor is supported by a wooden frame that's sitting on the ground. In the middle of the space is a tiny patch of cracked and broken concrete. No wonder this room is cold and damp and the house gets moist. He then walks me through the medieval garden-party room to the kitchen and shows me the other floors all have a concrete base because they're tile. I get it. He wants to put a concrete base under this floor as well, and he wants to build it into the *devis*. Why not?

"Bon," I say. "Oui."

Two days later I bring all the paperwork to the insurance guy with great trepidation. I walk into his office and expect him to shudder. He leaps when he sees me, comes around his desk—the first time ever—and shakes my hand. Then he guides me to a chair and sits me down, none of which I think bodes well. The only times I've seen him this happy is when I was leaving. I figure he's comforting me, easing me into the bad news.

He starts right in talking about the flood—*l'inondation*—the rain, storm—*l'orage*—and the dam that didn't hold. He explains this to me making hand gestures and wooshing noises, punctuating everything with "C'est dommage," "dommage," and "une catastrophe." The more he goes on, the more I wonder how much I'm going to lose—all of it, three-quarters, half, a third? He's so happy, I can't tell. I wait for him to finish, then hand him my papers.

He takes them, reads them quickly, nodding, saying "Bon, bon, oui." French people hate to deliver bad news. They'll do anything to avoid it. I'm sure he's putting on the happy face—it's the happiest I've ever seen him—to tell me no, I don't qualify. It was an act of God or some such thing and, as with all insurance, you're covered for everything except what you claim.

This is what I'm thinking as he removes a piece of paper from the drawer in his desk and starts writing. He makes a list of all the items I've claimed. Next to each item he writes the cost I've claimed. I don't know if this is good news or cruel and unusual punishment. He draws a line down the page and rearranges the list into two columns. Over one column he puts a ^. Over the other a -. I figure ^ means I get a pittance and - that I owe him. He writes 100% over the ^ column and 80% over the - column, and I see it's worse than I thought, a total loss.

He turns the paper toward me and says, "Normalement," and I want to cry. He points to the items with a ^ and explains they will be covered 100 percent. The items with the - will be covered 80 percent. I look at the lists. The 100 percent coverage has to do with the minor costs, the hours of work for cleaning the house, and the mileage for driving to the dump and to Quimper to get the rugs cleaned. The 80 percent coverage has to do with serious damage, which includes replacing the floor and the concrete slab. Twenty percent deductible, given the price of the floor and the concrete, leaves a substantial cost for me.

I start to argue, telling him the floor is new, less than a year old, beautifully finished, and I show him the bill, "Regardez," and the date of the work, "Regardez," and photos, "*Regardez*," and underline in red how much I paid.

"Non, non." He shakes his head, emphatic, beaming, even happier than he was before. He turns the paper toward himself and draws another line creating a third column and adds a + everywhere there is a -.

"Qu'est-ce que c'est?" I ask, intrigued. This is either a good thing or a tax—an *additional* tax they've added to my deductible.

"Le supplément."

"Quel supplément?"

"Le supplément pour l'inondation."

"Combien?"

"Vingt-cinq."

"Vingt-cinq percent?"

"Oui."

"Vingt percent deductible et vingt-cinq supplément?"

"Oui."

"Cinq percent plus le facture!"

"Oui."

"Pourquoi?"

"L'inondation."

I don't get it and I don't care. I'm getting five percent more than the bill I've submitted. It's incredible. I shake his hand and I stand to leave. I'm even happier than he is—another first. I've never left an insurance agency with more money than my claim. I'm joyous and all in favor of state regulation of insurance, when he tells me two things: (1) I have to wait for the inspector to approve the claim, and (2) I need to go to the *trésorerie*, the tax office, in Loscoat. My first thought is I'm screwed—they're going to give me a five percent supplement and make me pay the twenty-two percent value added tax on my entire claim. Then I remind myself all of my business dealings so far—with the bank, *notaire*, oil and floor guys, even the insurance guy—have been fair, honest, and positive, and have turned out well for me. Why shouldn't this be the same? Just because it involves insurance doesn't mean it *has* to be bad. This isn't State Farm or Allstate.

I wait for the inspector, hoping for the best and fearing I'm becoming delusional. He comes in a week, shakes my hand, spends ten minutes, and approves everything, including the new concrete base for the floor. He even points out a space in the closet under the stairs where there's no concrete under the floor and builds it into the coverage. Who would believe it? Proactive, preemptive insurance. If the house floods again, the damage will be less and so will their cost. What a country!

Still, I don't want to go to the *trésorerie*. What good can possibly come from going to a tax office? I wait until I'm too afraid of what will happen if I wait any longer—interest, fees, penalties; I'm forced to sell my house at auction. I open the door and say, "Bonjour." Nothing else. I'm deadpan. If this *is* a tax, I want them to know I'm not happy.

For all it matters, I'm not there. The lady behind the counter out deadpans me. "Votre nom?"

"Monsieur Greenside."

"Carte d'identité."

I show her my checkbook and California driver's license. She hands me an envelope.

I'm here. I have my checkbook. I might as well save the postage. I rip open the envelope to see what the damage is, how much I owe, and remove a piece of paper that looks suspiciously like a check. It has my name on it and *deux milles francs*, about $320.

"Qu'est-ce que c'est?"

"Un chèque."

"Pourquoi?"

"L'inondation."

Now I really don't get it. The insurance guy gives me a five percent supplement and the village gives me $320. I don't know what it is, but I like it. If this is how insurance is handled in France, I'm thrilled. I can't wait to make another claim. Meanwhile, I have a beautiful new chestnut floor with a new concrete base underneath it and the cleanest wooden furniture legs in France.

After that, I gladly pay my insurance bill, though I never know when it is due or how much I owe because I never receive a bill. Sometime in mid-January I wake up panicked, thinking, my God, my insurance has lapsed, I'm not covered, there's going to be a disaster—eighty-five percent of France's energy is nuclear—I'll lose the house, and I send him a check for last year's amount. He always sends back a confirmation letter thanking me as only the French can, in long, sweeping, sincere sentences telling me I owe him more. I then send another check and he sends the same letter back to me and that's the end of it for the year—only this time along with the second thank-you letter is a brochure with information about some new service I now have in my homeowner's insurance, lucky me.

In the U.S., I never read these notices when I receive them. But in France, where I can't understand a thing, I'm curious and scared, curious about what it means and scared there's bad news hidden in it somewhere and I better find out.

I have three options. I could ask Monsieur and Madame Nedelec, both of whom read and speak English fluently, but they work full-time, have very full lives, and take everything I ask them very seriously. If I bring this to them, they will research it, check the library, the Minitel, make phone calls, and spend hours making sure they have everything right. I don't want to ask them to do it.

Option two is Jean and Sharon, who also are fluent in English—but they are lefties from the sixties, *soixante-huitards*, and they dislike and distrust "the system" even more than I do. *I* look at the French health system, social security, unemployment, all of the human resources provided by the state, and I marvel. *They* look and see diminishing returns. All of us, I know, are right. Once I said to Jean, "There are more gardeners here than cops. I *never* see the police, even at large public gatherings." He said, "*You* don't see them, but they're everywhere." If I bring this to Sharon and Jean, I'll be even more frightened about what it says and what *they*, my insurance company, could do.

Option three is Madame P, who doesn't speak English but has the patience of Job and Sisyphus combined. She explains that as a result of having homeowner's insurance, I now have traveler's insurance too. The enclosed brochure provides an example: Monsieur C is traveling abroad with his family, for example in England, where one of them becomes ill—because of something he ate; she laughs. This insurance pays for the necessary care in England, then flies the person back to France for real treatment as soon as he is able to be moved. As an insured homeowner in France, I have this protection, because, as Madame informs me, I am Monsieur C.

I'm delighted, but does it apply to me, a U.S. citizen? I ask Madame, who asks Monsieur. They confer and conclude, "Yes. But of course. You live in France. You're paying for the insurance, how could it be otherwise? En principe . . . Normalement . . ."

I decide to ask the insurance guy. I open his office door and say, "Bonjour." He looks cheerful, almost happy to see me, but not quite as happy as last time, because last time he knew what I wanted to discuss and this time he doesn't, a situation guaranteed to raise the anxiety of French people. "Bonjour," I say again, shaking his hand and sitting down.

"Bonjour." He smiles, but he's wary, so I get to the point, which makes him warier still, because it's those little pleasantries about the sun, cold, weather, rain that puts everyone who knows how to speak French at ease. Since I don't, I start right in. "Bon," I say, "Je suis Monsieur C."

He looks at me and nods, though he clearly knows my name is Greenside.

"Par example."

"Oui."

He's looking more and more dubious, wondering, I can see, if this is some sort of fast-talking, city-slicker American trick. To put him at ease, I remove my insurance card from my wallet and hand it to him. He scowls, then takes a sheet of blank paper from a pile on his desk and writes my name on top: Greenside. I get it. He thinks the American's making another claim.

"Non, non, une question."

I hand him the brochure that was mailed to me and point to myself. "C'est pour moi?"

"Oui."

I point to the example. "Je suis Monsieur C?"

He stares at me.

"Par example. Je suis dans les États-Unis et j'ai une grande malade. Vous êtes revenir moi aux France, le même aux Monsieur C?"

"Oui. Bien sûr." It's a testament to French fortitude or intuition that no one attempts to correct my speech.

"Mai j'habit aux les États-Unis tout la jour."

"Oui."

"Par example. C'est Décembre. Je suis dans mon maison en Californie et tombe et casse mon tête. L'assurance payee pour l'avion revenir moi aux France?"

"Oui. Absolument."

"J'aime beaucoup France," I say, shaking his hand and standing up to leave. I have no idea how they do it—making loans to strangers to buy a house, covering medical expenses, paying insurance claims as they do—but it's wonderful and the right thing to do.

It's in this spirit of being truly grateful that I decide to tell him I rent my house, it's a business, and I know I'll have to pay more for insurance.

I walk past his office several times over a two-week period, trying to get the gumption to tell him the truth and voluntarily pay more for my insurance. I'm also waiting to see him alone in the office, not working with someone else, because my French is so bad every encounter takes a lifetime. I find out later he thought I was stalking him, walking past his office, not waving or stopping, peering in. When I finally open the door and walk in, he leaps out of his chair and greets me with more enthusiasm than I've ever seen.

"Bonjour," I say, shaking his hand and taking my customary chair, facing him. I proceed to make small talk, about the weather, sun, coolness, clouds, to put him at ease, but I can tell I'm making him warier: like, He always just gets to the point, why doesn't he get to the point . . . So I get to the point. "Bon. J'ai une question."

He flips through the in box on his desk and retrieves my file, which is odd. Usually he has to get it from the file cabinet. The fact that it's on his desk tells me he's been waiting for me. I proceed carefully, knowing I'm on dangerous ground.

"Je louer la maison."

"Ouiiiiiiii." He's buying time.

"Je reste ici un pur et après louer la maison."

"Ouiiiiiiiiiiiiiiiiiiiiiiiiiiiiiii." He's not giving an inch.

So again I ask the question that I'd never ask in the U.S. and still causes me wonder. "C'est nécessaire je payee plus?"

"Pourquoi?" He's as puzzled as I am. Who is this guy who keeps wanting to give me money?

"Je louer la maison."

"Ouiiiiiiiiiiiii . . . Combien du temps vous êtes ici?"

"Deux mois maximum."

"Deux." He holds up two fingers.

"Oui."

He removes a blank piece of paper from his desk and starts writing. He turns to his computer, pulls something up and reads it, is about to explain it to me and, stops. Why bother? He turns on the adding machine, enters a lot of numbers, goes back to the computer, prints it all out, and hands me the paper. The difference is 600 francs, about $100. "Bon,"

I say. Not bad. I expected much worse. The price of honesty is $100, something I can afford. I take out my checkbook. "Je payee maintenant."

He shakes his head in disbelief, wondering how I survive at all. He underlines the figure and hands it to me again.

"Oui. Six cents francs. Je payee maintenant—ou vous êtes prefer par envoie?"

He closes his eyes in dismay, disappointment, despair, who can tell? "C'est réduit."

"Réduit?"

"Moins."

"Moins?"

"Oui. Je vous paie." He's smiling again, beaming, relaxed. It's over, he thinks, and I'm going to leave.

"Pourquoi?"

His face falls. It takes him a full thirty minutes to explain to me that while I am there, all of my belongings—personal things like cameras, computer, clothes—are covered. But when I'm not there, the personal things of my renters are not covered. The house is covered, the furniture, my stuff is, but theirs is not. The result being *réduit*, a reduction, something I've yet to see in the U.S. In the U.S., I get new savings on my car insurance every year—for not smoking, not having any tickets, no accidents—and with every good driver award, my rates go up. Not in France. It's another wonderful difference between a regulated and free enterprise system.

I've now seen my insurance guy in France ten times more than I've seen my insurance guy in the U.S. I understand about one-third of what he says to me, which isn't much less than when it's explained to me in English. I know I scare him, my insurance guy in France, but I figure it's better that I scare him than for him to scare me, which is how it is in the U.S. I dread calling my insurance guy in California, but in France, my insurance guy dreads me. Who can blame him? In the U.S., I'm afraid to make a claim because if I do my rates will go up or I'll lose my insurance. In France, I've made four claims, two for cars, two for the house, and everything has been 100 percent completely covered. There has been no cost to me, no outrageous deductibles, no lawyers, everything has been promptly paid. In the case of the flood, they paid more than I claimed, all of which is absolute proof that a regulated economy will destroy my freedom.

A few days before I return to California, I see him in the Bricomarché. I'm shopping for a new kitchen faucet. He walks past my aisle in a hurry, heading in the direction of paint. I follow him to say, "Bonjour, au revoir, merci, and à bientôt," but can't find him anywhere. It takes me a while to realize he's probably avoiding me. I understand. I often feel that way too. I think about "accidentally" finding him to tell him it's okay, but if I do I know he'll feel worse. I go back to plumbing and leave him wherever he is, the winner. I buy my faucet, take it home, and wait for Martin or Jean to install it.

Martin and Jean

Martin is English from Cornwall, partnered to Louise from Guernsey. Jean is Breton from Nantes, married to Sharon from Montreal. They—Martin and Jean—are as different as England and France.

Jean is an intellectual—a *French* intellectual—thin, slightly hunched and slouched, with longish graying hair, black-framed glasses hanging from a string around his neck, smoking, wearing frayed sweaters and shirts, always grumbling about the U.S., the French government, society in general, the way of the world. He can explain quantum theory and semiotics and quote Nietzsche, Spinoza, and Lao-tzu in English and French.

Martin is a hunk, all sinew and muscle. Shirt off most of the summer, muscles rippling, lifting, hauling, pushing, banging—everything with him is physical. He speaks with an Australian accent (he lived there for a while) that's harder for me to understand than French. Every woman who visits me wants to talk with Jean and sleep with Martin, which doesn't make Louise or Jean very happy.

Jean broods, worries, thinks, stays in his house, which is in the country, for days at a time. Martin is a party guy, social, funny, a drinker, boater, beacher, sun guy, going out every chance and moment he has. He drives a classic Indian motorcycle and a cherry 1938 Renault that he works on and maintains himself. Jean drives a twenty-year-old 4CV Renault van that he put together from two other 4CV Renault vans he's cannibalized and stores at his house.

"Everything is crap" to Jean. "Nothing works right. It's all garbage, not worth fixing," he says, as he fixes it, because the thought of replacing it with something new makes him feel worse.

With Martin, everything's "No problem." The stairs wobble. "No problem." There are moles in the yard. "No problem." And even when there is a problem, like it's nine o'clock at night and he's run out of glue or tape or paste, and if he doesn't immediately stick down what he's working on everything will come undone, "No problem." He manages with something else.

Jean overstates and exaggerates impending doom and failure and collapse, inherent being and nothingness. Martin understates the problem. No matter how serious it is he tackles it with enthusiasm, as if it's one more stop on his way to the beach. Martin apprenticed in England as a stonemason, Jean in France as an electrician and sound man for films. Both have traveled extensively, and both built and designed their own homes: Jean from an old barn, Martin from an uninhabited, dilapidated stone wreck. Each did everything—roof, floors, walls, wiring, venting, plumbing, windows, garden, heating, chimneys—and did it completely differently.

Jean wastes nothing, buys as little as possible, and fabricates whatever he can: tools, parts, furniture. Tin cans become lampshades. Flattened, they're windowsills. Bent, they're troughs feeding rainwater to Sharon's kitchen and living-room gardens. The house is insulated with empty wine bottles and cut-up tires cemented into the walls. The love seat in front of the fireplace is the backseat of a 4CV Renault. When he replaced the roof on his house, he hand-cut hundreds of pieces of slate using traditional tools and set the pieces in a six-part diagonal pattern, not because it's pretty, which he couldn't care less about, but because it's the best pattern for keeping out moisture and bats. He built his own windows, including the frames, using found wood and old glass he salvaged from somewhere. Jean is French, yet a John Stuart Mill–like utilitarian to the core.

Martin is French country chic. His house is like a *manoir* or hunting lodge with modern comforts and conveniences built in everywhere: a shelf here, drawers there, a closet, storage area, window, light, sliding door, extra toilets. The rooms are spacious and everything is spectacularly finished, including the ceiling beams, which are stained and varnished with a secret product Martin invented to bring out the texture and color of the wood. Walls are newly plastered and painted or covered with period wallpaper. Floors are refinished wood, pointed old stone, and newly laid tile, all refurbished and refitted by Martin.

Jean has a mental plan, a blueprint for everything he does. When he builds a window, he wants to understand the properties of the wood, the glass, silicone, the zinc shielding, the weather, the direction of the wind, rain, and sun. He wants as few surprises as possible, knowing they are always there. Martin operates in reverse. He looks at something and knows exactly what it needs. He begins and lets the process lead him to the end. Jean starts with the end. Having both of them as friends willing to help me with my house is a miracle.

One morning I turn the burner on to heat water to make coffee and I smell gas. It's my worst nightmare, far surpassing overflowing septic tanks, leaky roofs, bats, and burst pipes. It's primal, taking me back to Grandma Esther and her pleading admonitions to get electric, not gas, when we moved to our house on Long Island. "It's not safe," she said. "You can't smell it, and then you explode." She meant: gas chambers, Zyklon B, and Nazis—don't do it.

I turn the burner off, put my nose on the tank, run it along the rubber hose connecting the tank to the stove, and smell nothing. I turn on the left rear and left front burners and smell nothing. I turn on the right front burner, the one I started with, and smell gas. I turn it off, shut off the tank, and wait.

Martin is still in Australia, not yet in Plobien. My choice is to call Madame P, whom I've already called about the oil tank and everything else, or Jean. I decide to follow Kipling's advice and share the burden.

"Bonjour, Jean."

"Hello, Mark."

"I think my stove's broken. I smell gas."

Jean doesn't waste his time asking me questions. He knows whatever I say will be useless or wrong. He arrives in fifteen minutes, carrying his tools in his handmade wooden toolbox, knowing I won't have what he needs, or if I do, it will be crap and break while he's using it.

"The tank and hose are okay. I checked," I tell him.

He turns on the tank and smells it, then the hose. I don't blame him, it's his life too, but I feel vindicated when he smells nothing and restrain myself from saying, See.

He turns off the gas and begins dismantling the top of the stove. I *know* he's fixing it, and I *know* I called him, but it feels like a violation, like I'm betraying the stove—I tend to anthropomorphize things—by subjecting it to this operation. Those are my first thoughts. As the parts pile up, I have second, third, and fourth thoughts—all of which center around What if I've found the one thing in the world he can't fix?

I go upstairs to the bathroom to ponder this question. When I return Jean's got the knob off and is testing the electric starter with an ancient, huge, wooden-boxed meter that looks like it's right out of *Frankenstein*. It wouldn't surprise me if the stove came alive. "I don't know," he says to the meter, "This stove is old, dangerous . . . impossible to find parts for. . . ." It sounds hopeless, futile, easier to find the lost ark. In my mind, I'm already walking the aisles shopping for a new stove at Leclerc, Brittany's answer to Costco.

Meanwhile, Jean's unscrewing this, removing that, making notes and diagrams to remind him this minuscule thingie that looks exactly like that minuscule thingie, but is not exactly like it, goes here. Finally, he locates the problem: a hairline crack in a linguini-thin pipe that feeds gas from the burner to the jet. He begins to dismantle the burner. "I don't know," he says to the burner. "I don't think this will work. I don't think I can fix it. I think you'll have to get a new stove." *I* think I should have called Madame P for an artisan.

I'm ready to end this torture, call it quits, thank him for his effort, offer him a beer, wine, a pastis . . .

"Do you have a tin can?"

Oh God, please, not with a tin can! I'm going to go boom, I know it. Grandma Esther, here I come! I rummage through the garbage and find an empty can of corn niblets. There's a zillion acres of corn growing here, and all of it is for chickens. Humans get their corn in a can.

"A can opener?"

That's it. I'm dead. I hand it to him with visions of myself all over the walls. I watch as he opens and removes the bottom of the can, making it open-ended. I watch as he cuts the can from top to bottom and flattens it on the table. "I don't know if this will work," he says to the can. "I don't think so." *I* don't either. I watch as he snips a two-inch piece of tin from the flattened can, places a nail in the center, and carefully, meticulously, as if rolling a cigarette with his last shreds of tobacco, rolls the tin around the nail, once, twice, thrice—*Et voilà!*— a tube, a pipe—a sleeve!—that he slides over the old broken pipe, covering the crack, and creating a new connection. Holy cow! Maybe I won't have to buy a new stove or die.

He solders the sleeve in place, saying, "Maybe it will work. I don't know. I don't think so." Then he turns on the gas, smells, sniffs, puts his nose all over the burner and the pipe and shrugs, telling me we just entered the world of fate, that what happens next is beyond his control, we're either going to die or we're not. He takes out his lighter: I take a step backward. He lights it and runs it over and under the sleeve. There's no boom. We're still here. He turns the burner on, and pop, it ignites! I'm amazed. There's no fire or explosion, and I don't need a new stove. "I don't know," he says to his lighter, "I think maybe you need a new stove." He puts everything back together and tests it all again: the burner, hose, connections. Then he accepts a beer and leaves.

Every time after that, the first thing he does when he comes into the house is go to the stove and ask, "It still works?"

"Sure," I say, "*You* fixed it."

He checks the hose and burners to make sure. "I don't know. It's okay now, but it's not going to last."

Jean works like a sleuth. His favorite tools are a stethoscope and his huge, old electric meter. For him every project is a problem, a puzzle to solve. For Martin, it's an enemy to destroy.

Martin's last enemy before he moves to Portugal (for more sun and beach and sea time) is the building of a two-foot-high, fifty-foot-long stone wall in front of my house. He's already changed the attic from an inquisitor's delight into a cozy, comfortable, four-skylight, beamed loft bedroom with tile bath. He's replastered and painted every wall in the house and redesigned the kitchen, adding cabinet space, a new sink, and well-hidden dishwasher. He cut a hole through the three-foot-thick stone wall in the medieval garden-party room to make a door that opens onto the slate patio he designed and built, which faces the river. He's stabilized stairs, replaced the gauges and knobs on the radiators, and repointed all five fire-places. There's not a part of the house he hasn't worked on and no material he cannot handle. But working with stone, building a wall, this is Martin at his best, what he's actually been trained to do: stonemasonry.

For a week people have been walking and driving past the house to watch him work—*French* people: the same people who won't look through an open door or window when they walk past are walking and driving here to observe his work. From morning to dusk, he hammers the stone, breaking it, fitting the pieces together, matching color, shape, size, and texture. He holds the pieces in his hands like cards—this one, this one, this one, not this one, working for six straight days. Tomorrow he leaves for Portugal, where Louise is waiting, and I leave for California.

I'm cleaning the house for the renters who will arrive in two days. I'm on my fourth and final load of laundry when the washing machine jams—again! It's the third time, and I'm beginning to think this machine was designed with repair in mind. The first time it jammed I called Madame P, who called her younger son, Henri, and his wife-to-be, Renée. They spent three hours taking the machine apart screw by screw to unjam it. The second time I didn't have the nerve to ask Henri and Renée, so I asked Madame P to find someone else, and she called Monsieur Robert, who also spent three hours taking the machine apart screw by screw to unjam it. The only good thing about *this* jam is Martin is here.

"Martin, what do you know about washing machines?"

"Nothing, mate."

"That's more than I know. Mine just jammed, would you look?"

Reluctantly, he puts down his hammer and walks to the shed. He opens the outer door of the machine and tries to turn the drum. It's cement-stuck. He bangs it, tries to force it, leverage it, make it do what he wants. He shakes the machine, turns it on its side, actually lifts it, trying to shake it or jar it loose. It sounds to me like the machine is crying. He starts banging really hard, turns it completely over. Sweat's pouring out of him, he's cursing. He hates this job, hates getting nowhere with it even more, and hates not finishing the wall. After fifteen minutes he turns it upright, sets it back where it was, and says, "Call Jean."

"Bonjour, Jean."

"Hello, Mark."

"My washing machine's jammed."

He arrives in ten minutes, holding something that looks like a hanger. When he gets closer I see it is a hanger. Martin sees it too, and stops hammering stones and follows him. Jean opens the outer door of the machine, sticks the hanger in the space between the tumbler and the rubber wall and jiggles it, catches the latch, and turns the drum far enough so he can reach in and remove the clothing piece by piece, until he can turn the drum fully and free it. "Wow!" I say. "Thanks," and start to refill the machine.

Jean stops me. He picks up two squares of wood, places a piece on each side of the latch on the inner door and bends the latch forty-five degrees, an angle that ensures he'll never have to do this again. "I don't know," he says to the machine. "It won't last."

Martin slaps Jean on the back and says something neither Jean nor I understand. Then we walk to the wall so Jean can see what Martin's done. He walks the length of the wall, all fifty feet, front and back, stopping here and there to better observe. "It's good," Jean says, as he says about all of Martin's work. It's the greatest compliment Jean gives. I go into the house and return with three beers. We sit on the wall enjoying the end of the day, the summer, the last time the three of us are together.

Martin's left me a house that has been Martinized and a beautiful stone wall that people still drive by to admire. Jean's given me, among many things, a washing machine that not only works but may be the only one besides his in all of France that is jam free. Without these friends, and Sharon and Louise and Madame P and her family, and later Monsieur Charles and Christine and John, I'd still be living in the Stone Age. It's another thing I like about my life in France. I'm grateful.

In the U.S., where I'm relatively successful and know how to get what I want, I'm often angry and frustrated—especially by long lines, traffic, and automated telephone-answering systems. But in France, where I'm helpless and child-like dependent on others, an anathema to any adult U.S. male, I'm grateful. I'd never say it aloud (for fear of losing it) or tell anyone (I'd be embarrassed), but my days in Brittany are days of grace.

A Day in the Life

In Oakland I live in the hills at least thirty minutes from most of my friends, not near or convenient to anyone, so they're reluctant to visit. Brittany, however, twenty hours away plus a thousand-dollar plane ticket, doesn't seem to pose any problem. I understand completely. If any of my friends bought a house in France, I'd want to see it, and if they told me the stories I've been telling them, I'd want to discover what's real.

Their visits begin my third summer, the second after buying the house—already I'm counting like the French. LeRoy, my roommate for ten years, plans a ten-day tour of World War I battlefields—Verdun, the Marne, Amiens, the Somme, Ypres, Argonne, the Meuse—and I join him. Joanna, who's fluent in French—this is my new dividing line: once it was virgin, nonvirgin, then it was progressive, not progressive; now it's speaks French, doesn't speak French—decides to rendezvous with us after her *Backroads* bicycle trip in Provence. The plan is to meet at the house. If she gets there first, she's to go to Madame P's, get the key, and wait for us, which is what happens. She opens the house, airs it out, takes a shower, goes shopping for dinner, and begins a load of wash. The last is her first mistake.

In France, very little is convenient or easy. To this day, I cannot open French packaging without a screwdriver or knife. Anything that says "New Package" or "Easy to Open," I avoid, the way I do restaurants named Mom's in the U.S. I follow all directions faithfully. I carefully cut along the white dots prominently displayed on the flap of cardboard attached to the box of soup, believing this time I'll create the perfect spout exactly as it's outlined on the box. I cut diligently, a surgeon, gaining confidence with every snip. I finish and gently squeeze the box, ever hopeful, expecting to form a spout. The soup dribbles, drips, shoots into the pot, over the counter, the stove, and me. I have yet to successfully peel the tinfoil from the mouth of a container of milk. I try, always fail, and wind up punching it through with a knife and spilling it. I've ripped half a roll of toilet paper looking for the seam. Nuts and potato chips fly out of their packages like freed wild birds. But the worst is plastic wrap because it's ingeniously disarming. It's the only box I *can* easily open, but then it's impossible to locate the edge of the plastic. Lately, they've begun placing a piece of blue tape over the lip to help identify it, and it does help, but it still takes four hands to use it, otherwise it jumbles, sticks, and wads. And if, through some manipulation I'll never be able to duplicate, I'm lucky enough to actually free a usable sheet of plastic, I make the mistake of yanking up, as in the U.S., instead of down, as in France, and use ten times more than I need. I'm beginning to think that's the point. The packaging forces you to waste and mishandle the product, which forces you to buy more of it sooner. That seems to be the logic behind it, the raison d'être, as well as perhaps building manual dexterity and inuring you to the absurd, frustrating, and diabolical. In its own twisted way, it makes sense.

The washing machine does not. What's even more baffling is that it's not French but German—Brandt. All I can figure is it's a special version they export to France to get back for Alsace-Lorraine. Take Joanna, for example. She's a middle-aged American woman with several advanced degrees. She speaks French, Spanish, English, Indonesian, Tamil, and Vietnamese. She's traveled to the remotest parts of Asia alone and flown and survived Garuda Airlines. She has thirty years of successful experience doing laundry, all of which would lead any reasonable person to believe she could also do laundry in France. Ha! Working the washing machine here is like trying to use the plastic wrap with one hand.

Why? Because the Germans, in their revenge, designed a washing machine with two doors, an inner and an outer, and a drum that turns from top to bottom, not side to side. The clothes go in the drum, which unfortunately is thimble size, so it holds about one-third of what a typical Kenmore holds. Also, unfortunately, the machine doesn't operate with hot water, though Germany and France do have hot water, but for some reason not for this machine. No, the *machine* heats the water. What's the difference? About an hour and a half! Each one of these tiny, thimble-sized loads takes between an hour and a half and two hours to complete, depending on how hot you set the water. The temperature can be set at 30, 60, or 90 degrees. It's centigrade, so Americans set it at 90, forgetting 100 is boiling, and all the colors bleed. But these are only minor inconveniences, none of which is the cause of Joanna's problem.

She put her clothes in the drum, and, world traveler that

she is, intelligent, sage, and successful, she sets the temperature gauge at 30, shuts the outer door, turns the dial, and thinks she's going to wash her clothes. But she's not. Either she's forgotten to close the inner door because no other machine in the world has two doors, or she's remembered, but the latch—this is before Jean bends it—is built in such a way as to release at the slightest tension, which, *quelle surprise!* a drum full of dirty clothes more than amply provides. The door opens—*Voilà!*—and since the drum turns from top to bottom, the clothes pop out on the first swing down and jam the drum, which stops the machine, but not the cold water. That requires turning the machine off, which Joanna does.

Her first response, being a capable, can-do American woman, is to fix it, but she can't. Her next response is to pour herself a glass of wine and wait for LeRoy and me to arrive. She knows us well enough to know we can't fix it either, but since it's my house she expects I'll know whom to call—and that she'll see her clothes again sometime this summer. She takes a chair and her glass of wine from the house and sits on the grass under the quince tree, watching the sailboats and swans float by.

LeRoy and I arrive at six o'clock, greasy, exhausted, and salt-and-caffeine-wired, after an eight-hour, several times getting lost, four coffees and Cokes, three *grandes frites* each drive from Amiens. All I want to do is get out of the car, shower, sit on the lawn, and sip wine.

We greet with quick pleasantries and California hugs, then LeRoy and I carry our bags into the house, LeRoy to the pre-Martin, still unfinished, nail-infested attic, me to the second-floor bedroom. Joanna's bag is in the second-floor study. I unpack and shower. LeRoy does the same. An hour later, feeling civil if not civilized, I go downstairs and find Joanna in the kitchen reading a cookbook. In front of her, on the table, is the largest bird I've ever seen, complete with head and feet and two huge crowns of purple garlic. "Who's your friend?" I ask.

"Poulet noir," she says, then tells me about her clothes and the washing machine.

Immediately I go into action. I call Madame P. I fly through the few salutations I know, "Bonjour, ça va, beaucoup soleil, bon santé," then blurt, "Machine à lave est kaput. C'est marche pas. Pas de tournée, au revoir," and leave it at that.

You'd think by now they'd change their number or stop answering the phone, or at least screen their calls, but they're French and too social to do that. Twenty minutes later Madame arrives with the troops: Henri and Renée. Both are about nineteen. Neither inspires much confidence. Still, whatever they know is more than I know, and if they can't fix it, *they* will know whom to call.

Joanna, LeRoy, and I follow Madame, Henri and Renée to the shed to watch them. Joanna, I can see, is thinking she's never going to see her clothes again. I'm thinking my washing machine is gone. LeRoy's thinking about dinner. Renée unplugs the machine and detaches the hoses, and together she and Henri lift it—it's as heavy as a Panzer and wreaks as much damage—and carry it to the lawn. Renée finds the plug and drains it, then they lift it again and put it down on a dry spot and begin to circle it. LeRoy, Joanna, and I join the circling. Madame decides to make use of the time by working in her garden, which is half the front yard of my house.

After much circling and discussion Henri asks me, in English, for a screwdriver and pliers. I have them because every house should have them, not because I use them. Henri takes the screwdriver and gives Renée the pliers. In five minutes,

these two easygoing kids have become world-class disman-
tlers, hopefully not demolishers. They're taking the machine
apart screw by screw. I cannot believe this is German designed.
It has to be Italian. French. English. I can't watch anymore. I
know I'm going to have to buy a new machine tomorrow, and
probably a new wardrobe for Joanna as well.

We leave them on the lawn unscrewing things and go to
the kitchen, LeRoy and I pretending to help, when Madame
P comes in and says something to me, then remembers who
she's talking to and takes me by the hand to the garden. I think
she wants to show me her radishes or how the green beans are
growing, or some type of lettuce she knows I'll think is a weed
and destroy, but she doesn't. She points to the sky and says
something.

"Oui," I say, as I always do in France when I don't understand what's being said. In English I say, "No?"

She goes, "Zzzzzzzzzzzzzzzz," and pinches me. Hard.

"Ow!" What is this—some secret French greeting, the
Breton version of noogies, my punishment for not speaking
French? She points at the sky again, and I see a bunch of bugs
flying over the house. In the U.S., I kill anything that flies into
the house that's not a bird. In France, land without screens,
I'm inured. Flies enter and leave the house on the ground
floor, mosquitoes and bees on the second floor, and bats on
the third. Something buzzing *outside* the house doesn't bother
me at all, but it certainly does Madame. She goes into the
house and explains it to Joanna.

"Bees," Joanna says. "Les abeilles. There's a hive in your
chimney. If you start a fire and upset those guys, you're in
trouble."

Now what? It's 8:00. Henri and Renée are on the lawn, dismantling my washing machine. Madame is in her garden dig-

ging potatoes, radishes, onions, leek, and zucchini. Joanna's trying to figure out when to put the bird in the oven. LeRoy's reading *Herald Tribune* box scores, and I've got bees swarming my house. I walk over to Henri and ask him what I should do.

"Call the pompiers."

"The pompiers?"

"The firemen."

"Bon." If they can get cats out of trees in Oakland, why not bees in France? I call. "Bonjour."

"Bonsoir."

Already I'm wrong. "Je suis Monsieur Greenside."

"Oui."

"L'Américain au Kostez Gwer."

"Oui."

"J'ai l'abbée," telling them I either have bees or an abbey.

"Oui."

"C'est possible vous êtes visit mon maison ce soir?"

"Oui."

"Bon."

Thirty minutes later, they arrive in full regalia with a truck, hoses, ladders, all of it. If there's a fire anywhere, those people are doomed. Three firemen and a girl exit the truck, spot Henri and Renée on the lawn, walk over, and shake their hands. Then they walk to Madame and shake hers. They look at me and say, "Bonsoir." Doing their job is one thing, familiarity and friendship another.

"Bonsoir," I say, and point to the chimney.

They look up and immediately start arguing. They walk closer to the house. The girl starts making hand motions as if surveying and gauging. Then one guy walks over to Henri and Renée, says something, and they all return to the truck and leave. I don't get it. I walk over to where Renée and Henri have the innards of the machine laid out like a museum display. Joanna's clothes are in a pile on the grass. It looks promising, though I have no idea how they will ever remember where each piece goes. "What's with the pompiers?" I ask.

"They brought the wrong size ladder."

"All that equipment and they have the wrong size ladder! What if there'd been a fire?"

Henri shrugs.

Renée begins the reassembly.

Joanna wants to know if she should put the chicken in the oven.

I shrug.

LeRoy grouses about the A's and the Giants losing.

Madame never stops digging. She has a pile of potatoes, shallots, zucchini, and lettuce, large enough to feed a village.

The firemen and girl return in the same truck, I hope with a different ladder. They exit quickly and make the rounds, shaking hands, including me this time. They look at the sky, the house, the chimney, the trees, the light, the clouds, and when they're finally ready—who knows why?—they remove the ladder from the truck, lean it against the house, and send the girl up to do the job. She scurries up, takes a look, and scurries down. This is followed by more discussion and walking around. Then the same guy as before walks over to Henri, says something, and they all leave.

I walk over to Henri and say, "Now what?"

"It's too early."

"It's after nine o'clock."

"The bees are too active. They'll come back later when they're sleeping."

"Okay," I call out to Joanna, who's back in the house. "Put the chicken in the oven. What the hell."

By 10:00, Henri and Renée have the machine almost back together. Madame's car is loaded with veggies and flowers. Joanna sticks her head out the window, "Dinner in fifteen minutes." Henri and Renée lift the machine and put it back in the shed.

"What about that?" I say, pointing to several small parts left in the grass. Henri shrugs. Renée says nothing. I think, Tomorrow I'm buying a Whirlpool. They plug in the machine, screw on the hoses, turn the dials, push the buttons, and fill it with Joanna's clothes. Before I can stop them, they've got both doors closed, inner and outer, and the machine is washing.

"C'est un mirac," I say. "Merci, merci beaucoup."

They both shrug. It only took them three hours. We go into the house to celebrate—beer and *apéritifs* all around. At 10:30 the chicken is done. Joanna takes it out of the oven just as the firemen return. We all go outside and watch the girl climb up the ladder in full protective wear, like medieval garb, and remove the hive with the now sleeping bees, who will wake up tomorrow in a new home. The hive is placed in a sack. The ladder is returned to the truck. The whole thing is completed in less than ten minutes. I offer to pay them for the trouble, but they refuse, telling me it's their job. I offer a tip, which they also refuse, saying, "No prob-lem, no prob-lem." I ask Henri what I should do. "Give them three hundred francs—fifty dollars—for beer." I do, and they accept it with lots of "Bonne soirées," and shake my hand, teaching me once again there's always a right way and a wrong way to do things in France, and I'd better learn the difference soon.

Joanna invites Madame, Henri, and Renée to dinner, and, as I expect, they decline. They just spent three hours helping me and didn't think anything of it, but coming into my house, meeting my friends, and sharing a meal is a level of commitment they don't have the energy to make. Henri and Renée have to work the next day. Madame has a carful of hydrangeas and veggies and Monsieur waiting for her at home. We walk them to their cars, thank them profusely, exchange many, many cheek kisses, and wish them "bonne soirée, bon nuit, bonsoir," and wave, *à bientôt.*

It's 11:00, dusk, when Joanna, LeRoy, and I sit down to a forty-garlic-clove chicken dinner with Madame's lettuce, shallots, potatoes, and green beans. We finally make it to our respective beds at 1:00 a.m., exhausted, but satisfied and full in every way. The next day I wake up early and go to the shed to check the washing machine and Joanna's laundry. The machine's fine, and so are Joanna's clothes—if pink is her favorite color.

The New Yorker in Me

One of the things I like best about my house is its location—
it's at the end, or beginning, of a village of about five hundred
people. The land behind the house is an open field maintained
by a herd of sheep. The land in front is a small, narrow, public
park that borders on the river. On the other side of the river
trees grow and men fish for salmon. A quarter mile beyond
the house the river turns wild in its run to and from the ocean.
It sounds like the boonies, but it's not. I have neighbors on
both sides, each side separated by a strand of thirty-foot-tall,
dense, dark green, billowy cypress trees that block my view
of their houses and their view of mine. I treasure these trees,
their majesty, their tree smell, their wooooshy sound in the
wind, and, of course, being from the U.S., the privacy they
afford, the sense of isolation without actually being isolated.
Two houses north is a restaurant.

Soon after I buy the house, the neighbor on the restaurant
side and a younger adult woman I've never seen before visit

me. This is rare in France. Strangers, meaning anyone you have not formally met, even neighbors, do not just drop by, and here they are, at four o'clock on a Sunday afternoon, after their *midi* family meal, before *goûter* and their evening *apéritif,* heading down my driveway. I know the man is my neighbor because I've seen him working in his garden, and I've shouted "Bonjour" and "Bonsoir" numerous times to him and his wife and their dog as I drove past them on my way to somewhere. I know I should have stopped and introduced myself, but after that what could I say? Nothing. So I drive past them waving and yelling, "Bonjour" and "Bonsoir," hoping to avoid another conversation I won't understand. And now he's here with a woman I've never seen before, knocking on my front door. Somehow I know they're not the Breton Good Neighbor Society.

I half-open the door and peer out. They're standing side by side, looking unsure but resolute. He's trim, mustachioed and silver-haired, wearing pressed white slacks, a forest-green shirt, and shiny oxblood shoes, looking very dapper, as if he dressed especially for this occasion. She's very pretty with short, dark, fashionably cut hair, wearing a yellow floral dress and low heels. I'm wearing cut-off jeans and a T-shirt that once was white and now is pinkish gray with a mustard stain on it from my ham sandwich lunch. Once again, I feel like an affront to the village, France, and humanity.

"Bonjour," Monsieur says, visibly hesitating, seeing it's worse than he expected, probably wondering if I'm contagious, and bravely extends his hand to shake. I put out my hand, say "Bonjour," and shake his. He nudges the woman to do likewise. She does, and we do. Then we all stand there not sure what's next. I'm waiting for my cue from them. They are waiting for me. It's my house, so I open the door and say,

"Entrée," and point them to the library–sitting room. They head straight for the couch, refusing to look at anything else, and huddle together, expecting the worst.

"Une boisson?" I ask. "Un bièr, pastis, jus, de l'eau, thé. Un café?"

They refuse everything.

An unannounced visit by people I don't know, who won't accept a drink, is not a good sign. I'm in trouble, but I have no idea about what. Monsieur begins speaking—in French. I recognize a few words: sun, trees, garden. I respond with my usual, "Ah, oui . . . Oui . . . C'est vrai . . . C'est joli," not understanding a thing. I think I'm doing pretty well listening to him, hanging in there, being friendly and neighborly, when he switches to English and says, "This is my daughter. She speaks very good English to you."

I know what this means: we'll fail to communicate in two languages instead of one.

"What my father's been saying," she says in perfect English, "is he wants you to cut your trees. They are green and very pretty on your side, but on our side they are brown and ugly and dead. Also, they hide the sun from the garden."

I sympathize. I do. I like the sun too, but I *don't* want to cut my trees. I offer a compromise. "I'll trim the trees. I'll cut two meters off the top and remove all the dead, brown branches on your side."

That's when she tells me about French law, a subject I've learned to dread. "In France," she says, "your neighbor—us—*we*—have the right to have any tree on your property that's within two meters of our property cut to two meters in height. . . ." I picture my beautiful trees, thirty feet tall, stumped to six, and remember reading something about the French and trees, and how they don't like them: nuts are okay;

fruit; flowers; a windbreak, a forest for hunting, even a pre-
serve, all are necessary. But a tree, in and of itself, per se, who
needs it? It's a mess, a bother, a potential hazard or problem,
work. The French, so romantic and nostalgic, sentimental, in
some ways, in others are more practical than the Brits.

I understand perfectly what she is telling me: they have the
right to force me to cut my trees.

We talk for a few more minutes about the weather, rain,
and the upcoming village fête. Then they stand, in unison,
and I walk them to the door, where we all shake hands again
and wish each other "bonne journée."

In the fall, I have the trees topped and the dead branches
facing their house removed. I do it every year, and over the
years, we become close friends—Louis and Jocelyne, their
daughter, Marie, their son, Jules, and their spouses, Léon and
Alexandra, writing, exchanging gifts, sharing meals, playing
boules, eating crêpes, hiking together, walking the beach,
drinking Ricard, visiting with each other, being invited to
family affairs—and never discuss the trees again.

That's how it is, until the day Jocelyne tells me she's selling
her half of the house to her brother, Pierre. As soon as she
says it, I know it means trouble. Living in France has done
this to me, made me fearful of change, *conservative*. I don't
know if it's as Marx said, because I'm a property owner, or my
tentativeness as a foreigner, but whatever it is, I've come to
believe change, almost any change, is not for the better but
the worse. In the U.S., I live as if there is nothing that cannot
be improved. In France, I don't touch a thing. I leave it alone
even if it is worn, bent, crooked, scratched, dented, if it skips,
blinks, it doesn't matter, because bad as it is, whatever I do
will make it worse.

Jocelyne sells her share of the house to her brother and his wife, Denise. Now, instead of a second home that the whole family shares at holiday times, it's a primary residence for one family to live in most of the time. When Jocelyne first told me, I worried. When I see Pierre, huge, muscular, always smiling, a retired cop, I panic and wait for the worst, but it doesn't happen. There's no knock on my door or angry, nasty looks as I drive by and call out, "Bonjour" and "Bonsoir." I begin to relax. Through friends I hear Pierre occasionally complains about the trees, but he isn't complaining to me, so I ignore it. It's the easiest I've ever had at playing dumb.

We "bonjour" and "bonsoir" our way to good neighborliness, at least that's what I'm thinking, until the summer I arrive and find a six-inch-wide swath of orange Day-Glo paint cutting across all of my trees at two meters' height. I don't know French, but I know what this means.

The next day, under cover of early morning darkness—like a commando or terrorist—with flashlight in one hand and a meter in the other, I sneak outside to measure the distance between my trees and Pierre's property, and see it's not necessary: the trees are within inches of his land. I ask Monsieur and Madame P, who confirm the two-meter law. I call Jean and Sharon, who say, "It's the law, you're in France, the trees are a pain, you should cut them." I speak with Monsieur and Madame Nedelec, who are outraged. Monsieur begins a search to see if perhaps this type of cypress tree is protected and finds it is not. He tells me to go to the *notaire*, the person who acted as the real estate agent when I bought the house from them, and ask if there's any legal recourse.

"Oui," he says after I draw him a picture of two houses separated by a row of trees and slash my finger across the trees, saying, "Coupe. Tout," and "J'aime beaucoup les arbes."

"Quel âge ont les arbres?"

How old? Jesus Christ, I don't know. "Je ne sais pas."

"S'ils ont trente ans, ils sont protégés."

"Oui!" If they're thirty years old, they're protected. I go back to Monsieur and Madame Nedelec and ask her, "When did your father buy the house? Were the trees there when he bought it? Did he plant them himself?"

Madame calls her mother. No one is exempt in this search. Her mother tells her her husband bought the house twenty-five years ago, and, yes, he planted the trees.

Relativity notwithstanding, twenty-five is not thirty, though Pierre doesn't know that yet. My plan is to ask the *notaire* to write an official letter to Pierre telling him about the thirty-year law and leave it up to him to prove the trees are not that old. I know if he searches he'll find the deed of the sale and maybe the truth about the trees. On the other hand, I also know French people hate coming into contact with the bureaucracy in any way—especially, especially with lawyers—and that a letter from the *notaire* in and of itself could do the trick.

Meanwhile, everyone in the village is talking about the trees, though not to me. Most people agree the law is on Pierre's side, no question about it, a neighbor has the right to see the sun. And everyone seems to know this law, like in the U.S. when people say possession is nine-tenths of the law. In France, they say a neighbor has the right. . . . Somehow I've walked into local lore, probably something that emerged from years of class struggle between wealthy landowners and small farmers, and I'm lining up with the lawyers and aristocrats, not exactly where I want to be, though, in truth, I guess that's what I am. Those who support me think it's not a neighborly thing to do, demand your neighbor cut his trees, and he, Pierre, should not have marked my trees with his Day-Glo paint. Property is property is property. He has the right to have the trees cut, but he doesn't have the right to touch them. It's another of those French paradoxes.

By the end of the summer, Pierre and I still haven't spoken, and I'm beginning to think it will blow over, as it did with Louis and Jocelyne and Marie. French people do not like social surprises or confrontations, and generally they think Americans are nice, but also crazy, meaning not predictable and potentially volatile, why else all those dead Indians and guns, so maybe he'll leave me alone.

Ha.

I pull into my driveway, the car filled with shopping bags. Pierre greets me before I get the first bag out of the car. We shake hands and he begins speaking the fastest French I've ever heard in my life. Any other conversation and I wouldn't have a clue, but this one, I know *exactly* what he's saying, though I act as if I don't, hoping he'll see I'm an idiot, take pity, and leave me alone. He takes my hand and leads me to the trees and shows me how ugly they are on his side—dead, brown—not like the billowy green on my side. He points to the sky and shows me the shadow on his garden.

Speaking as slowly as he can, which is still very fast, and using hand motions and moving his arms up and down, he lets me know he is offering to cut them, at his expense, and haul them away. He wants to eliminate them completely, no two-meter height, and replace them with a two-meter hedge that he will pay for, plant, and maintain. All very reasonable and proper, I think—and no way, not a chance, not with *my* trees he won't. I point to my head and say, "Je pense."

I have to come up with something fast: either the *notaire*

bluff letter or a compromise. What to do? What to do? I unpack the grocery bags and sit on the patio, sipping a Ricard and facing the trees, missing them even before they are gone. I have to salvage something, save some of them, because I treasure them and because Monsieur and Madame Nedelec bestowed the care of this house and property on me—I still think of it as really theirs—and I don't want to let them down. Sitting there, thinking about this, it comes to me.

I'll agree to cut the trees from the road all the way back to his garage. That way he'll get full sun on his garden, have a full view, and not have to see the dead, brown branches. The rest of the trees, from his garage to the back of the house, would remain. He has no windows on that side of his house and no backyard. The area between his garage and the trees is a storage area for a boat. Leaving the trees behind his house where he can't see them shouldn't be a problem.

I tell Madame and Monsieur P, and they agree it's fair. I tell Jean and Sharon. They think Pierre has the right to say yes or no. I tell Monsieur and Madame Nedelec. They say to try it, though I know they prefer I resist.

I go to Pierre's house in the afternoon, after *midi*, in the hope that he's relaxed and full and satisfied and maybe a little drunk from lunch, and explain my solution. I lead him to the tree next to his garage and say, "Ici, coupe," then walk forward to the road, and point. "Tout. Pas des arbres. Au revoir." Then I walk him from the same tree next to his garage in the other direction, back, and say, "La même. Pas de coupe."

"Non." He shakes his head and takes me to the border of our properties. "Deux mètres," and shows me the trees are within two meters of his property. Then he points to the orange Day-Glo swath, "Deux mètres," and shows me how much he's allowed to force me to cut. "C'est le droit." It's the law.

I'm furious but don't have the language to express it, which is probably for the best.

The next day Martin stops by. We sit on the patio he designed and built, drinking Ricard, watching the sailboats float through the lock, when it dawns on me, I should ask *him* to speak with Pierre. Martin is fluent in French and knows Pierre, likes him, has spoken with him many times—and being English, is not reluctant to get involved in personal matters, especially personal matters involving the French. I ask Martin to explain in detail, in French (as opposed to my hand motions and single words) that I see Pierre's point, and I want to address his problems and take away the ugly view and the shadows on his garden—and how the trees *behind* his house do not affect him at all. He won't see them, *can't* see them, and they won't block the sun from his garden. It's fair. Reasonable. A win-win—and I'll pay for everything, cutting the trees, removing them, and building and maintaining a new, two-meter-high, wooden fence. Reason and cost, two things I'm sure will prevail in France.

Martin agrees to try. I refill our glasses, and we wait for Pierre to come outside and work in his garden as he usually does in the late afternoon. Thankfully, he appears before we're completely sloshed. Martin and I walk over to him. I'm hoping to resolve this amicably, though Martin has already told me, (1) it is fair and reasonable, and (2) Pierre won't go for it. He explains the whole thing in great detail—how I want to be a good neighbor, pointing to the sun, Pierre's garden, the trees, making sweeping motions with his arms, laughing, joking, all of it very friendly and going, I think, very well. As soon as Martin finishes, Pierre says, "Non."

He makes his own sweeping motion with his arms and says "all of them." "Tout. C'est le droit."

Something pre-Lascaux churns in me, and my own personal double helix does a flip. I tap Martin on the shoulder, and as calmly as I can, with my most friendly and reassuring smile on my face, nodding yes, yes, yes to Pierre, I say, "Tell him this: if he makes me cut all of my trees, I will plant something in *my* yard, *more* than two meters from his yard, that will grow so high and so fast he'll *never* see the sun again."

The effect is incredible. In zero seconds, Pierre goes cold, becoming the least animated French person I've ever seen.

"Tell him," I say to Martin, "C'est le droit."

Ten minutes later we have a deal: I'll cut and remove all the trees—about ten of them—from the road in front of his house to his garage, and replace them with a new fence that Martin will build and install. The rest of the trees will remain as is. We shake—all three of us—and it's a deal.

Two days later I give Pierre a bottle of Ricard to seal the deal and thank him for being reasonable. The following week he gives me a huge bowl of langoustine that he and Denise bought from a fisherman on the coast and seasoned and cooked for me. After that we exchange pleasantries and gifts regularly, though he still speaks so fast I can barely understand him. What *he* thinks of what *I* say, I can't even imagine.

For a while I avoid sitting on the patio. The missing trees are like ghost limbs. Sometimes I think they're still there. Eventually I return, though, because even with their loss it's beautiful, especially in late afternoon. I sit there when it's not raining, in the bright, unfiltered light, watching the river flow, sailboats pass through the lock, and the sky. It's like being inside a bowl or a planetarium, where everything above you is immense. It's on one of those late afternoons, I see that Pierre was right: the view and light and openness without the trees are better for *me*, as well as for him. I sit there, embarrassed by the fuss I made, then drive into town to buy a bottle of Ricard and do something I've never done in the U.S. I give him the bottle and tell him he was right and thank him for being a good neighbor—*un bon voisin*—and for making me a good neighbor too. Living here surprises the hell out of me.

Île Callot

When Donna and I begin dating seriously all my friends are thrilled and delighted. None, I imagine, more than my Breton friends, who undoubtedly sing, "Free at last, free at last, thank God Almighty, free at last," now that someone else is responsible for me. Ha!

Donna is Japanese-American, from the Minamoto clan, a group of people so resolute they make the Anglo-Saxon stiff upper lip look like a simper. These people *will* themselves to death when they think their time has come, and if honor is involved, they die even sooner. Once, when I was sick with the flu for four days and convinced I had everything from mono to yellow and rheumatic fevers, Donna asked me if I wanted a bowl of noodle soup from the local Chinese restaurant. "Sure," I groaned from the bathroom, where I'd made my living quarters. "That would be nice." It was 9:00 a.m. when she asked, 10:00 a.m. when she left, and 5:00 p.m. when she returned and handed me a container of lukewarm wonton soup.

"Where were you?" I asked. "I expected you at noon."

"I had to get out of here. Your whining was driving me nuts."

Whining! I thought I was a brick, a regular Judah Macca-bee, but she saw me as a Jeremiah. Little wonder. My people have been getting their kishkes squeezed out of them for millennia, running and hiding, fearing the knock in the night. Hers have been slicing and slaughtering anything that moved in Asia, including themselves. It's an interesting match.

In very white Brittany, Donna's exotic. People walk up to her and touch her hair—physical proximity and the need to be tactile being much greater in France than in the U.S. If a stranger touched Donna in the U.S., she'd clobber him. In France, people she doesn't know stop her on the street and ask, "What are you?" She always answers, "American," and they always respond, "No, no, what *are* you?" not satisfied until she says, "Japanese." Then they smile and the conversation begins. French people like to know who they're talking to. It's only then that they know what to say. That's why all those rules and right and wrong ways of saying everything.

One of the things that moves me to tears is Donna's morning salutation, "'Bye, honey, I'm going to work.'" It brings joy to my heart: she's the only girlfriend I've had who's been gainfully employed. That's the good news. The bad news is she's *self*-employed, which means her vacation time is limited. I'm always careful to have my housey chores and responsibilities finished by the time she arrives so we can take little one-, two-, and three-day trips to places I've been and want to show her, or places I've never been and want us both to see. That's how we discover Île Callot.

———————

We're on a two-day trip along the North Atlantic coast, starting at Le Conquet and ending at Roscoff. I go against my better judgment and try something new. Instead of taking the direct route, the route I'm familiar with, I drive inland, to Saint-Renan, a village I've never heard of. It's written in large, dark letters on the map, situated with all roads leading in and out of it, making it a hub, a hub in the middle of nowhere with a traffic jam like the L.A. and L.I. expressways combined.

"Let's stop," Donna says.

In the U.S. I'd resist, wanting to get to our destination, but this is France, and it's market day, and we're not going anywhere.

I park like the French, on the sidewalk. The market's everywhere—on both sides of the main street, in alleys, the park, around the church and *mairie*, in front of the *pissoir*—and everything imaginable is for sale: beds, window frames, dressers, chairs, vacuum cleaners, tools, kitchenware; clothes for kids, young women, middle-aged women, old women; shoes, hats, sweaters, T-shirts; live animals, dead animals, cooked animals, raw animals; whole and filleted fish, snapping crustaceans, flapping fowl, chunks of mammals, pizza, paella, nuts, flowers, veggies, fruit, olives, cheese, spices, wine, cider, beer, pastry, cake, and every kind of sausage imaginable. We buy a hunk of white bread cut from a loaf the size of a truck tire, local cheese, a tomme and chèvre, dry sausage with pistachios, pâté de campagne, strawberries from Plougastel, two pears, two green apples, a bottle of local cider, and a huge chocolate truffle for dessert—and drive to Pointe de Corsen on the Atlantic for a picnic.

We arrive at one o'clock. The French have another hour to eat, so parking is easy. I unpack the food and a blanket and set it all on a large, flat rock overlooking the sea. It's perfect—

gentle breeze, waves cracking, a royal blue sky with white Rorschach clouds, and we have it all to ourselves—until an entourage from a local wedding arrives for a photo shoot. I've seen French wedding pictures in window displays. The groom, twenty years old, smiling and happy, the proud captain of his ship. The bride in her gown, standing on the rocks, the waves and turbulence behind her. The bride and groom together, safe on the shore. It's the French at their most nostalgic and sentimental, turning the moment into a permanent Renoir, forgetting for the moment Picasso and Toulouse-Lautrec. Donna and I watch the photographer shoot picture after picture, moving the bride and groom a little this way, a little that. When she's finished, I toast them with our bottle of cider. Donna wishes them "Félicitations, bonne santé, et bonne chance."

We finish eating and clean up—better than the French, but who's comparing?—and drive to Le Conquet and the Hôtel St. Barbe, where we have reservations for the night. Upon seeing the hotel, I have additional reservations. It's 1920s pre-depression depression faux-Mediterranean, with a cracked façade and faded, peeling, dingy, colorless paint. Donna looks at me and I shrug. I know what she's thinking, because I'm thinking it too—bleak room, lumpy bed, no shower—or worse, one of those dribbly things on a hose that wets you one body part at a time while the rest of you freezes.

I carry the bags into the hotel lobby and sing "Bon-jour" to the dressed-in-black, string-bean-thin, middle-aged woman behind the counter, like I'm happy as hell to be here. "Je suis Monsieur Greenseed. . . ." For some reason I've recently decided this is how my name is pronounced in French. "J'ai une réservation. Chambre deux, quatre, deux," I say, and hold up two, four, and two fingers for clarity. It's the room the guidebook says to reserve. Donna shakes her head and walks away, suddenly compelled to read a poster announcing a Vivaldi concert that happened a month ago.

"Ouiiii," the lady says. "Voudriez-vous une réservation pour le restaurant ce soir?" She points.

I look to my right into a blindingly bright, modern, windows-on-three-sides, hanging-over-the-Atlantic dining room. "Est-ce possible un table à côté la fenêtre, madame?"

"Non, monsieur."

I'm not surprised. I've been in France long enough to know the customer is *never* right. Still, I ask, "Pourquoi?"

"Vous avez la chambre, pas de table."

Seems fair enough. No one should get everything. "Bon," I say, "à huit heures."

She writes it down, hands me the key, and points toward the elevator. I drag Donna away from the poster, which she's now reading as if it were written by Proust and she'll be tested on it later. We take the elevator to the second floor and follow the signs toward room 242, out the old building, into the new. Ours is the last room at the end of the hall. I insert the key and push open the door, and it's like stepping into space, flying, and floating over the sea. The room is glass from ceiling to floor on two sides. To the right is the busy fishing port and harbor of Le Conquet; facing us, pummeling the cliffs, is the Atlantic.

Donna walks around the room, saying, "Incroyable, incroyable."

I follow her, checking things out. The toilet and shower are new. There's even a glass shower door to keep the bathroom from getting soaked when we bathe, something every country except France seems to have mastered. The reading lamps have 60-watt bulbs instead of the normal 25- and

40-watters—and they work! I sit on the bed, expecting *this* to be the corner that's cut. "Holy cow! It's comfortable. We lucked out. It's like being at sea *without* being at sea and getting seasick."

We leave our bags in the room and go for a walk on the coast road, oohing and ahhing over the jagged, rocky cliffs, turbulent sea, towering sky with its palpable light, and the ubiquitous relandscaping by Hitler: concrete bunkers and pillboxes cut into the cliffs at every cove, inlet, and peninsula as far as the eye can see. It's sobering enough to drive a person to drink, which is what I intend to do at dinner.

Back at the hotel, I shower first and leave the bathroom to Donna. I've decided to dress for dinner, meaning I'll wear a shirt with a collar, clean pants, and socks instead of bare feet with my sandals. That's the plan. The problem is, I left my towel in the bathroom, and my clothes are in the suitcase on the floor in front of the window on the other side of the room, and I'm naked. I could knock on the door and ask Donna for the towel, but why bother her? We're on the second floor, this is France, I've seen more nudity on the public beaches and family TV than in R-rated movies in the U.S. If anyone sees me, who cares? I'll never see the person again. I tiptoe across the room toward the suitcase. A woman on the port side waves to me. What the hell! I've got nothing to be ashamed of. I move closer to the window and wave back—with all of me.

At dinner, she's at the table next to us. She doesn't give the slightest hint of recognition, which the American me is not sure is a compliment, but that's how it is in France. The public is often private (men peeing alongside the highway, and passersby pretending they're not there), and the private is often public (using the right utensils, sitting in the right place, serving the right food in the right order, everything *propre*). I'm learning which is which by trial and lots of errors. The lady smiles at me as we leave. I smile back and wish her "Bonsoir."

We go back to our room, where I can't wait to see the night view. During dinner I kept looking at the sky as it darkened, but the lights in the restaurant were too bright for me to see very much. I push open the door and we're greeted by the ping . . . ping . . . ping of the foghorn followed by a lick of light from the lighthouse at the mouth of the harbor . . . Ping, ping, lick . . . Ping, ping, lick . . . The rhythm is soothing and romantic and so are the winking stars and waxing moon. We make love as if we're outside under the sky and moon and stars, only this is better, because we're not. There are no bugs. It's not cold. I can get up and pee in a toilet and fall asleep in a bed.

I wake at six-thirty and go downstairs for the normal ten-dollar, one-cup, no-refill-coffee, small—which they don't bother to call *grande*—orange-juice, half-a-baguette, two-croissants, quarter-pound-of-butter, and three-jam breakfast. Donna joins me, making it a twenty-dollar breakfast, then we leave. We drive along the Atlantic coast through heavy rain, sunlight, clouds, and drizzle, passing cows, sheep, the occasional goat, and wedges of traffic slowing, often blocking, Tour-de-France-look-alike, sixty-year-old and teenage bicyclists. We're going to Roscoff, where the guidebook says Mary Queen of Scots landed in 1548, Bonnie Prince Charlie in 1746, and today a daily ferry from Plymouth deposits its load of Irish, Scots, Welsh, and English. We drive to the terminal, take one look, and keep going. The next town is Saint Pol-de-Léon, the birthplace of Madame P. I've been there with her, and I want Donna to see the magnificent fifteenth-century Gothic spire of Notre-Dame du Kreisker, the tallest steeple in Brittany. It's from the top of the spire, standing in the wind, grasping the stone wall, exhausted and relieved after successfully climbing one hundred seventy progressively smaller and narrower railingless stairs, that Donna spies a tiny island with a sandy beach, a few houses, and a chapel.

"Let's go," she says.

I give her my Are you crazy? look, and see it means nothing to her, so I say, "Okay," and we're off to Île Callot.

I drive through the village of Carantec onto the one-and-a-half-lane road to the île. The only cars on the road are coming from the opposite direction. Donna mentions this to me as we arrive on the île.

"Great," I say, "no crowds." I'm even happier when I see there are only two cars in the parking lot, and both have their engines running.

We take the trail to the chapel over tumbling weedy hills and sliding sand dunes, past a few grand old wind-and-rain-worn ivy- and moss-covered stone houses, crossing immaculate, white, solitary beaches. What the hell do the people who live here do? I wonder. Donna wonders where they are. "Nobody's here," she says when we reach the top of the hill and the chapel.

I turn around, doing a full three-hundred-sixty. She's right. There isn't a person, bar-tabac, or *boulangerie* in sight. It's as if everyone knows some horrible secret, and we don't. I pull open the chapel door, half expecting the place to be full and everyone yelling, "Bonjour!" but it's as empty as everything else. We walk around, look at the altar, ceiling, posters on the walls, and out the windows at the roiling sea. Then we follow the trail back down the grassy hill, across the beach and the dunes, to the path and the parking lot. Our Twingo is the only car there. "I don't get it," I say, "such a private and beautiful place and no one's here." Donna looks at me in a way I choose to ignore.

We get into the car and I back onto the tiny road we came in on and turn toward Carantec, which is in clear view, less than five minutes away. The problem is in one minute the road I'm on—the road I want, the *only* road, the road Donna said as we drove in, "Why is everyone going the other way?"—that road is now under six inches of water. I open the door and look down. Water laps at the hubcap. I close the door and look at Donna. She shakes her head, No. It's five o'clock. I'm hungry, she's tired, there's no place to eat or rest on the île, and the tide won't change for another six hours—I gun the engine.

"I wouldn't," she says. "There's a reason no one else is here."

"Yeah, it's the difference between being French and American." I put the car in gear.

"Look!" She grabs the wheel and points to a group of people moving in single file and wedges, hikers with backpacks, kids, old people with canes and dogs, five or six cars, and a tractor crossing a spit of land, a tiny beach connecting Île Callot to Carantec. It looks like a procession at Lourdes.

"All right," I say, like I'm doing her a favor. Who knows how fast the water comes in, how deep it is, or if the road dips? I turn onto the beach and drive toward the crowd, and even though I know it's the right thing to do, it's abhorrent to my go-it-alone American spirit.

The car slides and slips over the rippling, pillowy, moving and shifting—I'm thinking *Lawrence of Arabia*—sand. I don't know if going faster or slower is better. Slower, I'm afraid of getting stuck; faster, I lose control. I floor the accelerator, pick up speed, and fishtail into a sand dune.

"Do you believe this?" I'm laughing like we're on a ride at Coney or Asterix or Disney. I put the car in reverse and go nowhere. I put it in first and stay put. Donna's laughing so hard she has to pee. People are watching us as if we're their favorite show—Martin and Lewis, two of the three stooges, Chevy Chase on Mr. Hulot's holiday. They're also keeping their distance, not offering any help or advice, as if whatever possesses us could also afflict them. I floor the gas pedal, barely manage to squiggle us out, and drive toward the tail of the procession, still laughing, as I pass a few older and lamer types hobbling along with canes. I pass a guy walking with his dog, wave out the window, and shout, "Au revoir."

"Get a horse," he shouts back and waves a happy farewell.

I'm almost at the end of the procession. The only thing that separates us from the last vehicle—the tractor—is a small rolling dune. After that, it's flat, hard-packed beach all the way to Carantec. I look left, and right. The dune runs the entire width of the spit. The only way around is over it. Donna looks at me, not certain if she should be concerned, but pretty sure.

"Don't worry," I say, "I have a plan. I'll follow the tire tracks from the other cars, and zip, we'll be over."

It's a good plan, and it would have worked, except the vehicles in front of us are vans and SUVs and large sedans and that tractor, all of which have much wider wheelbases than my Twingo. I floor the accelerator and drive straight into the dune and get stuck. I put it in reverse and gas it. Nothing. I try rocking it back and forth, still laughing and sputtering, "Stuck in a sand dune. How will I explain this to Renault? I lost the car at sea. I wonder if this thing floats." I don't know why I think it's a joke. I know we're on an île, *an island*, but for some reason I'm convinced this strip of sand stays above water. I'm still laughing when the "Get a horse" guy and his dog walk past.

"Monsieur," I say, giggling, "Combien du temps pour la mer?"

"Cinq minutes."

"Five minutes!"

"Oui."

Holy shit. I put the car in first and floor it. Nothing. I put it in reverse and floor it again. I'm going nowhere but deeper into the dune. The man and his dog step away from the car and watch. Up ahead, the guy in the tractor is crawling along. I do the only thing left. I hit the horn—just lay on it, hard, long, forever, and hope to hell the guy can hear it over the sound of his tractor and the now howling dog, and realize I'm not beeping hello, or worse, good-bye.

"I'll save you," Donna says, still laughing, knowing I can't swim.

I push the horn harder, as if somehow that will make it louder, then open the car door and stand there, hand on horn, hoping he'll turn around so I can wave for help.

Meanwhile, I'm thinking, "five minutes," how can that be? He must be joking. The sea is far enough away to not have to worry. Simultaneously, Donna and I point at each other and say "Pentrez," remembering the day we took a short walk on the beach, saw the tide zooming in, and ran back to our towels to find our clothes, including my wallet, in three inches of water, heading back to America without us. At Mont Saint-Michel, people drown every year because they underestimate the speed of the tide. This is serious, no longer a Hope and Crosby *On the Road* show, but a hope and pray.

The tractor guy finally turns around and sees me frantically waving. He stops his tractor and runs—races—the 100-plus yards to our car, like O.J., though hopefully not. One look at the tires and he understands. He and the "Get a horse" guy shake hands and discuss it. It's the quickest "what do you think" conversation I've ever heard in France. The tractor guy motions us out of the car and directs all of us, including the old guy and his dog, to lean against the car and push. The good news is the Twingo is light, and four adults and a German shepherd can move it. As soon as it's free, I jump behind the wheel and prepare the assault. The tractor guy goes nuts, jumps up and down, waves his hands, making stop, halt, Are you crazy! motions, and all but drags me out of the car. It's like a carjacking—like Monsieur Renault personally come to take back his car. He gets behind the wheel and floors it—in reverse. He backs up 25, 50, 100, 150 yards—a football field and a half. Anywhere else I'd think the car was a goner, he was stealing it—but his tractor is still there, on the beach where he left it, and is certainly worth more than my Twingo, which, in fact, isn't mine but rented.

We watch, Donna and I and the old guy and his German shepherd, as the tractor guy floors the Twingo and races toward us, like Le Mans, Monte Carlo, and the Grand Prix combined, and hits the sand dune doing at least 180 kilometers. The car wiggles left then right, wobbles, twists, and barely, just barely, hobbles over the dune to the other side.

The tractor guy leaps out of the car and waves—not even stopping to shake hands—and runs to his tractor. I pat the shepherd on his head, thank the old guy, and ask if he and the dog want a ride.

"Pas question!" he says. Who could blame him?

Donna and I get in the car, which is now covered with wet sand and seaweed, and catch up to the tractor guy, who's running to his tractor, not having the speed he did before. "Merci," I yell out the window. He waves to me. I point to the backseat, indicating I'd like to give him a ride. He waves me away like a swarm of mosquitoes circling his head. I pace him until he makes it safely to his tractor, trying to comfort him and assure him, let him know we're there for him if he needs us, but in retrospect probably terrorizing him with the idea we'd never leave.

I drive slowly in front of him, in case the Twingo dies or gets in trouble. Behind both of us are the old guy and his dog, walking. I drive straight into Carantec and stop at the first bar I see, so nervous my foot is shaking. My heart is pounding. Donna's so nervous she *can't* pee. We sit at a table on the terrace and I order two Ricards for me and one for Donna.

"Look at this," she says, looking at a photo on the menu. It's an aerial view of Île Callot totally surrounded by water: no road, no beach, no dunes, no spit of land. Nothing connected to nothing. I vow the next time all the cars are going in the other direction I'll do what Frenchmen have learned through the centuries: listen to the woman and follow the crowd. It's the start of something new in our relationship. What surprises me most is how easy it is to give in.

The Police

The police and I have always been close and never been friendly. I've been on the wrong side of them most of my life, even when I'm right—*especially* when I'm right, like protesting for civil, labor, and human rights and against war. I seem to bring out the worst in them, and the worst of the worst is at customs. I rarely cross a border where I am not stopped by one country or the other, sometimes both. I'm the only person I know who has been stopped by Canadians when I tried to enter their country. Canadians! Dudley Do-Righters! Who gets stopped by them? Me.

In the 1980s, I took a Greyhound bus north from San Francisco to Vancouver to visit a girlfriend spending the summer on Salt Spring Island. The bus stopped at the border and everyone descended, walking and joking through customs, declaring nothing, showing driver's licenses or Social Security cards or library cards—except me. I stepped one toe on Canadian tarmac and got pulled out of line for questioning.

"Passport."

"Passport? This is Canada. Who needs a passport?" Everything went downhill from there.

"Why are you coming to Canada?"

"Good question."

"How much money do you have?"

"Not enough."

"Where do you work?"

Terrorism wasn't yet a household fear, and the war in Vietnam was long over. No one was going to Canada to avoid anything, especially since everything to avoid was already there. Finally, for as little reason as they stopped me, they let me go—only my bus had already gone. I had to wait four hours for the next bus (sitting with the guy who stopped me and didn't stop anyone else, including a car full of Texans with rifles and beer in their trunk "for moose hunting") and another five hours once I got to Vancouver for the last ferry to Salt Spring.

On the other border, upon returning from a one-night stay in Mexico—in Ensenada—I was greeted at U.S. Customs with the customary welcome. "Put-your-hands-on-the-dash-board-of-your-ve-hicle-and-park-over-there."

"How can I drive over there with my hands on the dashboard of the ve-hicle?"

"Do it!"

I do, but it isn't easy. The car has a four-speed manual transmission. I get it into first by using my leg and knee and turn the wheel with my elbows, steering it close to the place he indicated, almost wiping out another border guy and his dog as I turn. As soon as I stop the car, the first border guy yanks the door open and orders me out, leading me to a tiny office where a guy three times human size asks me questions.

"Where were you in Ensenada?"

"Hussong's."

"What were you doing?"

"Drinking."

"Why did you go there?"

"Are you kidding?"

Meanwhile, I watch as my car is placed on a lift and lifted. I watch them lower the muffler and tailpipe assembly, search through the wheel wells, look under the hubcaps, remove the seats and door panels, and bring out the cutest little beagle I've ever seen to smell every inch of my car. That dog must be having a blast. The car is a thirty-year-old Volvo that leaks like a sieve and has mushrooms growing from whatever remains of the rugs. Two hours later, the car is reassembled, the dog is giddy, and I'm given a stern warning not to do anything wrong—or even think about it—and told, "We have your number." It's the friendliest thing anyone has said to me since I entered the U.S.

With experiences like these, not to mention reading Victor Hugo, Jean Genet, and Alfred Dreyfus, the last thing I want is an encounter with the gendarmes. If the U.S. and Canadian police treat me this way and I speak their language, I can't even imagine what French police would do.

It's June. I'm exhausted. I've just arrived at the house after an eleven-hour flight and a three-and-a-half hour wait in the airport—the normal hour and a half to get my luggage, and another two at customs, where the Africans, Arabs, and I were the only people stopped and searched. I open all the shutters and windows to air the house, leave my bags in the bedroom, and go out to start the car, the one Monsieur and Madame Nedelec gave me at the closing when I bought their house.

I don't have a garage, so when I left the summer before, I covered the car in plastic to protect it. I pull the plastic off and I'm shocked. The once blue paint is chipped, peeling, discolored. The car looks like it has impetigo, warts, rashes, shingles, and moles, and is devouring itself with Ebola. Even so, I'm happy. I have a car, and I don't have to spend the money I don't have to rent one.

I open the door and gag. Maybe I don't have a car. Under plastic for ten months, the last seven of which have been very, very wet, it's become a hydroponic greenhouse. Living things I've never seen before are growing in it. It *smells* alive. Monsieur and Madame Nedelec owned this car for ten years and it was fine. I own it for one year and have turned it into a tank of primordial ooze, the very source of life, which is great if you're a botanist or ichthyologist, but not if you need to drive, as I do.

There's nothing in the house. I *have* to go shopping, but the thought (forget the reality) of sitting in this car and touching anything, even breathing the air, is frightening and disgusting. If France is the mother of Legionnaires' disease, this could be the source.

I go into the house and find a piece of paper, scrunch it up into a ball, and hold it in my hand to protect me from the handle as I roll down the windows to let in fresh air, hoping I'm not giving whatever is living in there sustenance. I go back into the house and get an old beach towel, one I never want to see or use again, and drape it over the seat. Then I reach in, scrupulous about not touching or rubbing against anything, insert the key, and turn it. The engine starts immediately: Jean and Monsieur P have kept it running and primed all year—a task I now believe worthy of the Croix de Guerre. I touch the steering wheel with my pinkie. It's slippery-wet, sticky like snail goo. I go back into the house and find a pair of rubber kitchen gloves—pink, unfortunately—and put them on. Gloved and protected, I'm ready to go.

I back out of the driveway onto the one-lane country road. It's the road I drive every day, sometimes two or three times a day. I drive slowly, under the viaduct, marveling at the shimmering river, the exhilarating light, the sky, clouds, *vaches qui rit*, red-blue and white hydrangeas, trying to look inconspicuous in my pink gloves and blue-green Peugeot that looks like something resurrected from *Twenty Thousand Leagues Under the Sea*. As I drive I notice tractors, farm vehicles, trucks carrying pigs and chickens to market, the cars of people living in the rehab, social service apartments next to the *mairie*, poor people, recent immigrants and refugees from Turkey, and *everyone's* vehicle looks better than mine. Through the driver's side mirror I watch a car heading in the opposite direction stop, make a U-turn, and follow me. Even before I see him, I know it's a cop. He flashes his lights, and I pull over. Papillon, here I come!

The good news is he's stopped me in front of Monsieur and Madame P's house. If I scream and they understand me, I'm certain they'll come to my rescue. The bad news is I don't have my passport, don't speak French, and haven't the slightest idea why he's pulled me over.

I open the door and get out of the car. The cop seems startled, frightened. Clearly, I'm not from around these parts. I think about opening with "Je suis un propriétaire," and decide against it. My other two sentences, "C'est joli" and "Je n'ai pas d'argent," don't seem quite right either.

He gets out of his car and demands, "Identification."

I take off the gloves and hand him my international driver's license. He looks at me like, You've got to be kidding. I understand exactly how he feels: it looks to *me* like it came out of a box of Cracker Jack.

"Carte grise."

Luckily, I know that's the car's registration. I hand it to him. It has my name on it, the same name that's on the international driver's license. He takes both documents and walks to the passenger side of the car.

"L'assurance."

I remove the tiny green sticker that's attached to the front window—proof I have insurance—hand it to him and smile. The cop looks baffled. I'm not from around here, but I have a locally registered car and insurance in my name. He asks me questions, none of which I understand or answer. He's getting more and more frustrated. All he wants to do is extricate himself in a dignified manner. That's my cue. I smell it like a pig on truffles.

"Monsieur. Qu'est-ce que c'est?" What's up?

He blanches and takes a step backward, away from me. Obviously, nobody questions the gendarme.

"Monsieur!"

He starts to back away.

I follow, calling out, "Monsieur! Pourquoi? Je conduis—vous êtes arret moi. Pourquoi?"

He actually looks scared. "Nettoyez," he shouts. "Nettoyez, nettoyez—poubelle," two words I happen to know. He's pulled me over because my car is dirty. I don't know if this is police harassment or a French aesthetic critique—and which is worse. I do, however, form a hypothesis: French police get scared when they lose their authority and are out of control, and they'll do everything they can to avoid it. Shortly thereafter, I get to test it.

LeRoy, Rebecca, Donna, and I are heading south to the Dordogne. I'm driving. We're packed into a tiny Peugeot 106 we leased at the airport. I'm speeding along, feeling invincible. The car has red license plates identifying us as tourists, outsiders, foreigners—*strangers*. In Florida, this is a signal to kill. In France, it means leave them alone.

It's five o'clock. We've been driving all day. All we want to do is get to our hotel and rest. As we approach the village of Saint-Céré, I see several national police and gendarmes standing on the side of the roundabout, pointing at cars and pulling them over. In the U.S., when I see this I turn the other way. In France, with my red plates, I enter the roundabout with impunity.

A guy in tight pants and shiny leather boots, who would have been a hit in Nazi Germany or the Bois de Boulogne or the Castro, points his finger at me, then to the side of the road. As I get out of the car I say, "Watch this. This guy's going to be one sorry dude." I'm about to test my theory.

I close the car door and walk directly toward him, asking him questions in a French he's never heard and never could have imagined, even in his most Le Penian nightmares. The closer I get, the louder I get. I point to myself, the car, the road, the sky, shouting, "Qu'est-ce que c'est? . . . C'est joli. . . . Où est Sancerre?" The cop starts backing up. I keep advancing. He waves me away—points to my car, indicating it's a mistake. He's so anxious to get away, he leaps into the road and stops the traffic in all six lanes of the roundabout, creating a space for me to enter the road and leave. It's another of those cultural differences I savor. If I do this to a cop in the U.S., *I* disappear. If I do it in France, *they* do.

I now know the worst thing you can do to a French person is mock him. (Think of the movie *Ridicule*.) Public failure and humiliation are horrible things. Knowing this, I never ask people I know anything I think they won't know, because if they don't know, they will silently pretend they do and feel guilty—or worse, spend hours trying to find out, and *I'll* feel guilty, and I already feel guilty enough: for my French, etiquette, dress, dependence, the time they spend taking care of me instead of themselves, my perpetual need.

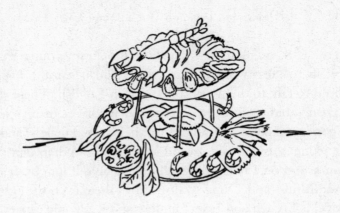

Bon Anniversaire to Me

I decide the summer I turn forty-nine that for my fiftieth birthday, in July, I'll give myself a party. It seems like a good idea at the time.

There's a restaurant north of my house, on the other side of Pierre's, with a bar and a banquet room for special events. I've never been inside, but I know the banquet room exists because on Saturday nights there are weddings and parties, and dozens of cars park in front of my house, and bad rock-'n'-roll and worse French rap blares until 3:00 a.m., when the celebrants leave happy, content, and drunk. And Tuesdays through Saturdays, scores of workers appear at noon for the forty-five-franc (nine-dollar), *midi* special, which lasts until 2:00 p.m., when the lunchers leave happy, content, and drunk. So I know the restaurant has the banquet room. What I don't know is how much it costs to rent and to feed my friends.

I put off asking because asking means going into the bar, which is the entrance to the restaurant, and having to speak.

In the U.S., going to bars depresses me. In my younger days, I went to meet women, but I never did because I was too afraid to talk to them—and that was in English. These days, I meet rabid, politically correct and incorrect drunks looking for someone to pummel with their stupid beliefs, and the someone is usually me. I wind up listening to their drivel for hours, and on a really bad night, hear myself join in. It's sad and pitiful—and I long to do it in France, even though the drivel is French and I can't understand it. People expect you to talk in a bar, even if it's drivel, *especially* if it's drivel. The person next to you or the bartender expects conversation and I don't want to be speechless or drivel-less with my neighbors and have them feel more responsible for my life than they already do. So whenever I see Stéphanie and Georges on the street or the quay or in the village, I sing, "Bon-jour," and keep moving, which is what I do the afternoon I return from a walk along the river and see Stéphanie pruning the roses, geraniums, begonias, and fuchsias that seem to grow from the restaurant's walls like Chia plants.

"Bon-jour, Stéphanie," I sing, and wave.

"Bonjour, Marc," she says, and then—who knows why? I look lost or thirsty or lonely?—she adds, "Voudriez-vous une boisson?" and points to the bar.

To say no would be rude. To say yes, I can't even imagine. "Oui," I hear myself say. "Merci," and start racking my brain for something to say to her.

I sit down, and she asks me what I'd like to drink. I know this is what she said because when I don't answer she pours me a big glass of red. I yearn to make small talk—drivel would be a godsend!—but after asking about her health, "Ça va?" her morality, "Vous êtes bien?" and the weather, "Beaucoup soleil, pas de plui," I'm done. So I ask about my party.

"L'année prochaine j'ai cinquante ans." I hold up two hands—five fingers on one hand, making a zero with the forefinger and thumb of the other. I do this because weeks before I asked for "cinq tranches jambon supérieur," and the woman began cutting *cent* slices. I stopped her at fifteen, and ever since I hold up my fingers like a four-year-old to indicate numbers.

"Ouiiiiiii," Stéphanie says, not sure if this is a joke, and if it's on her or me.

"J'ai voudrai un fête ici, dans le restaurant."

"Ouiiiiii."

"Combien le prix par person?"

"Ça dépend."

Here we go, from nice next-door lady offering a drink to a neighbor to bourgeois capitalist. "Pourquoi?"

She ignores me and asks, "Combien de personnes?"

I've counted twenty to twenty-five Bretons, but I have no idea how many Americans. "Quatre—zéro," I say, holding up four fingers with my left hand and making a zero with my right. Then I wobble my right hand, as in comme ci, comme ça, and say, "Cinq—zéro," raising five fingers and making a zero: forty to fifty people. That anyone does business with me is a miracle.

"Qu'est-ce que vous mangez?"

"Ça dépend."

She hands me several menus to look at. I see tête de veau (calf's head), andouillette (tripe), ris de veau (sweetbreads), boudin noir (blood pudding), andouille (pig intestine sausage), gésier (gizzard), and rognons (kidneys). I settle on a traditional four-course meal: *fruits de mer*, lamb or salmon with veggies and *frites*, green salad, and cheese selected by Stéphanie. "Pour le dessert, je va à la pâtisserie. Je achète le gâteau," I tell her.

She shrugs. The less she has to do with me the easier.

"Combien par person?"

"Cent francs."

"Et le prix pour le chambre?" I point to the banquet room.

"*Cent* francs par personne."

The total cost is less than twenty dollars a person—with the room. I'm thrilled, and I did it without being a total idiot, at least as far as *I* know.

"Qu'est-ce que vous voudriez comme boisson?"

Merde. I forgot the booze. Here's where she makes the killing. I point to the red I've been drinking, which is very good, and ask, "Combien pour ce la?" I don't even know if *ce la* are words.

"Quinze francs," she says, holding up one finger and five.

Holy shit, I'll go broke. "Par verre?"

"Par bouteille."

"Bon," I say, relieved. "C'est le même prix pour le blanc?"

"Non."

I knew it.

"C'est moins cher."

"Less?" I point down.

"Oui."

"Et du pain et le carafe d'eau, cent francs par personne?"

"Bien sûr," she says, trying not to sound doubtful and failing.

I give her the date and ask how much she wants in advance. "Combien avant, maintenant?"

Stéphanie looks at me like I'm testing her or teasing her, or I'm from Pluto, or the dumbest person on earth, and she's trying to decide which one as she slowly explains there is no down payment, letting me know by the way she says it that only an idiot would pay for something he hasn't received, and

I can hear in her voice that's she's begging, pleading with me to prove I'm not.

"Bon," I say, shake her hand and leave. The oil guy and floor guy didn't want any money in advance either. The bank guy was willing to give me a loan. At the gas pumps, I pump, *then* pay. *Everything* is based on trust. It makes no sense to me. For the rest of the summer, every time I see Stéphanie I ask if she wants any money. Each time, she brushes me away like a gnat.

At Christmas, I send invites to my friends in the U.S. I promise them a meal and a party and to put some of them up at the house, but the rest of the cost is theirs. Twenty-five say yes. I put eleven in the house, including Donna and me. LeRoy and Joanna are in the pre-Martinized, unfinished, nail-infested attic; Peggy and Larry are in the second-floor study, across the hall from Donna and me; Bruce and Bonnie are in the library–sitting room; and Gay and Stephen and their two teenage kids, Morgan and Nathaniel, are in the medieval garden-party room. Only the kitchen and bathroom—one bathroom!—have nobody sleeping in them. Mom and her friend Carol, whom I've known all my life, stay with Monsieur and Madame P so they can sleep and use the toilet and shower at will. Twenty-five Bretons also agree to attend, though when they find out I'm going to be fifty, no one really believes it. In Brittany, only widowers and crazy people live alone at fifty, and everyone knows I'm not a widower. I write to Stéphanie and tell her there will be fifty people for my fiftieth birthday and ask her if she wants a deposit. She doesn't respond.

By May, I begin to panic. Most of the French guests don't speak English, and most of the Americans don't speak French. One group or the other will feel slighted, and both of them will blame me. I'm going to create an international disaster

and lose friends from two continents. I decide to bring everyone together by placing the tables in a U with Monsieur and
Madame P, Donna, my mom, Carol, and me at the head. At
the sides I'll strategically place the bilinguals—Jean, Sharon,
Peggy, Joanna, Madame's son Henri—so everyone is within
shouting distance of someone to yell at.

I arrive in June and confirm with Stéphanie that the party's
on. "C'est bien?" I say. "Bien sûr," she says, like why wouldn't
it be? I ask her if she wants money. She looks at me like she
wants to say something, but doesn't.

"Bon," I say, "Merci. Je va à la pâtisserie. . . . À bientôt." I
can't tell if she's happy about the last part or not. I just thank
God these people like Jerry Lewis and the Three Stooges.
Anywhere else, it'd be a tragedy.

"Bon-jour," I sing as I enter the pâtisserie. I've never been
in the shop before, but I've been told it's the best in town.

"Bonjour," the woman says, looking at me so suspiciously *I*
wonder what I'm doing there.

"Bonjour," I say again, and head straight to the giant glass-
door refrigerator to look at the shelves of gorgeous desserts:
feuilletés, gâteaux, tartes of all types—cherry, strawberry,
apple, lemon, almond, pineapple, peach, pear—made with
meringue, chocolate, Chantilly, crème anglaise, crème fraîche,
fromage blanc, custard, mousse, and ice cream. They're elegant, understated, playful, celebratory, over the top; round,
square, rectangle; single, double, triple, septuple-layered. I'm
staring at them like a five-year-old.

"Monsieur," the lady calls, wanting to get me away from
the refrigerator, probably afraid I'll drool on the door.

"Oui," I say, and walk to the counter. "Je voudrai un
gâteau."

"Ouiiii."

No matter how many times I hear it, and I hear it a lot, it astonishes me how much disbelief the French can convey in one little affirmative "oui." "Pour un fête," I tell her. "Mon anniversaire."

"Ouiii."

"Cinq"—I hold up five fingers—"zéro"—I make a zero, "persons." To be triple sure I write it on a piece of paper: 50 persons.

"Oui." She then proceeds to show me several photo albums, like the floor guy and everyone else who's worked on the house, showing me example after example of her work, getting happier and friendlier with each page she turns. I decide on a lemon-blond two-layered cake with a raspberry center and chocolate icing. And for the decoration, she asks, almost smiling, flipping pages and pointing to cakes with happy couples, rockets, soccer teams, cowboys, boats, fish, cows, castles, indicating I can have anything I want, any kind of paraphernalia, edible or not.

"Non," I say, and the suspicious look returns. I hand her a piece of paper with the names of the fifty people who are attending. I printed the names so they can be easily read. "Tout," I say. "S'il vous plaît."

"Chaque nom?"

"Oui."

She looks at me, trying to decide if she should say what she's thinking: This is nuts. *You're* nuts. Do you know what you're doing? I've never seen this before. It's not the way we do things here. Then she shrugs. I'm a foreigner, probably a Brit, and says, "Bon."

I say, "Bon," and take out my checkbook and see I've done it again, breached all propriety, raised serious doubts about my competence to act, maybe even my species. I'm so embarrassed I'm afraid to ask her the price, but I'm thinking $150, maybe $200. I give her the date. She writes it down and tells me to pick up the cake next week, the day of the fête, at "Dix-neuf heures," and holds up nineteen fingers.

Every day that week I visit Stéphanie and Georges to make sure they have the right date, the right time, the correct number of people, the menu, the wine, the water, the tables, haven't double-booked. And because I'm a neighbor and not a widower, they answer my questions each time. I'd like to do the same with the cake lady, but she scares the hell out of me so I wait until the day of the fête, expecting the worst.

At seven o'clock, I go for the cake, foreseeing disaster: it won't be ready; it will look silly; the shop will be closed; the oven broke; the baker quit. I should have checked in during the week. I open the door and step in.

Sitting alone in the huge refrigerator, looking scrumptious and regal, is my almost black, dark-dark-chocolate-iced, wrinkled to look like drapery, lemon cake with fifty names in lavender, florid Louis XIV French script. Madame enters the shop, sees me, and calls her husband, the baker, and their son, the future baker. They stand there looking at the cake and smiling and talking—most of which I can't understand, though it's clear they're admiring their work. I am too. "C'est joli, beau, belle, bon," I say, hoping one of them is correct.

Madame ends it with a "bon."

"Oui. Bonne. Combien?"

She hands me the bill: three hundred francs, $50.

I pay her and leave, carefully carrying the cake to the car. "Bon anniversaire," she calls. "Bonne fête." She stands in the doorway, happier than I've ever seen her, waving and smiling as I drive away.

I bring the cake to the restaurant and give it to Stéphanie.

She looks at the names, at me, and decides to say nothing. Why bother? What does it matter? She's not responsible. "Bon," she says.

"Oui. Bon. C'est joli, n'est-ce pas?"

"Oui," she says, doing a pretty good imitation of sounding sincere.

She takes the cake into the kitchen. I peek into the banquet room. The tables, chairs, and name tags are in place. I see Georges and ask him for the one hundred tenth time if there's a microphone and tape deck. For the hundred tenth time, he says, "Oui." That none of these people has decked me is a testament to their patience, civility, neighborliness, and pity.

I go to the bar and wait to greet people as they arrive so no one feels any more lost than I do. Stéphanie sees me, pours me a glass of whiskey, and returns to the kitchen. I sit at the bar sipping, wondering for the gazillionth time, what the hell am I doing, and how can this possibly work?

The Americans arrive first, entering the bar like Normandy, and I see that it won't. They remove glasses from the tables, help themselves to the uncorked bottles of wine, and begin to roam the banquet room, the restaurant, the terrace, cross the street to the quay, the river, the park, and the lock, drinking, laughing, chatting, and returning for refills.

When the French arrive and see the Americans already there and comfortable, they become visibly dismayed, like they've committed some secret American etiquette gaffe, and they look at me as if I should have told them. They become even more dismayed when they see the Americans have begun drinking. This is not the beginning I'd hoped for.

The Americans roam aimlessly, obliviously happy—happy to be in France, in Brittany, drinking, taking space, chatting it up—like it's some kind of perpetual, endless happy hour where the drinks are good, plentiful, and free. The French are lost, confused, unsure of themselves, and self-conscious. They will not drink without food, and walking around with a glass of wine and not knowing where to go, what to do, or what's expected, makes them very uneasy. I watch as, family by family, they take matters into their own hands. They sit at the table, on the side of the U with their backs to the window, following their own cultural feng shui and ignoring the name tags. The Americans, upon seeing the French seated, scurry to sit down, worried they've committed some secret French savoir-faire etiquette gaffe. I rush to the head of the table and symbolically sit between Madame P and my mom. The French are on my left, the Americans on my right. It looks like the O.K. Corral. Then I notice Jean, my most anti-authoritarian *soixante-huitard* friend, sitting next to my next-door neighbor, Pierre, the ex-cop, and shudder.

I hurry to the microphone before anything bad can happen and welcome everyone in French, saying how pleased I am they are here. Peggy then repeats what I said in real French and Joanna repeats it in English because it's clear no one has understood what I said. I turn on the tape deck and play Josephine Baker singing "My Two Loves," my country and France. The Americans nod and get sentimental. Monsieur Jacques, a short fellow, like an elf, stands and informs me they're Breton, not French—and we're off.

Monsieur Robert, of lambig and venison pâté fame, who fixed the washing machine the second time it jammed, ambles over to where I'm sitting and whispers to me in French, "Servons-nous les premiers." It's a good idea. The first plate is *fruits de mer.* It will make the Bretons comfortable and happy and slow the Americans down, though that's not the reason he suggests it. The reason has to do with the significance of gesture: the right gift, touch, word, action—which in this case is the tangible demonstration of who's first.

I tell Stéphanie, who tells the two servers. The Bretons "bon" and "oui" when they see the plates piled with fresh clams, langoustine, snails, crab, mussels, lobster, and teensy things you pull out of their shell with a pin like earwax. It's a triple victory for the home team: not only are they served first, but they know what to do, and the Americans don't. What a party! Everyone gets to feel out of place.

The Americans watch the Bretons thoroughly and methodically disembowel and dismantle their food, cracking carapace, shells, and claws, snapping valves, scraping meat, breaking off the heads and thorax of the langoustine, and picking them and everything else dry. The Americans try to follow, but their side of the U looks like *Animal House*. They're splattered with crustacean juice and smell like sex or the sea. The Bretons are attempting not to gloat, and failing. Finally, the children take pity. Jean and Sharon's boys, Yann and Noé, circle the table, starting with Gay and Stephen's kids, and show the Americans how to break and enter the shells, eat the meat, and use the sauces. Most get the hang of it, though a few, like my mom, are disgusted. "You're lucky," I whisper. "The specialty of the house is tête de veau."

For the main dish, I ask Stéphanie to serve the Americans first. Monsieur Robert sees the first server come out carrying plates of salmon and lamb and deliver them to the American side of the table. He looks at me, disappointed, then nods, Okay. Fair is fair. I feel like I'm at Potsdam or Yalta with U.S. and Soviet troops sitting at the same table, at truce, but not in calm. The Americans are speaking English, the Bretons French. Each side watches the other eat, the different ways utensils are held, meat and fish are cut, knives and forks are used, Americans switching hands to cut and eat their food, Bretons looking at the Americans as if to say, Look, one hand! Mercifully, the wine is flowing and everyone is getting looped. People are on their best behavior, being polite and considerate, but staying with their own. It remains that way through cheese and salad: pleasant, formal, stifling. If I owned a watch, *I'd* be looking at the time.

At 11:30, Peggy goes to the microphone and explains in French and English that we're going to begin a roast. She says, "Roti," and the Bretons think it's another course and look at each other as if to say, After cheese?

LeRoy then stands and reads several letters he wrote and attributes to famous and prominent people, each of whom has something disparaging to say about me. The Americans howl. Peggy translates the letters into French. The Bretons are confused. How do I know Bill Clinton, and why would he say these terrible things about me—and why would my friends read them at my party?

Donna gets up and bangs two metal balls—*boules*—together, cracking jokes filled with sexual innuendo, no translation necessary. The Americans howl. The Bretons are aghast. You do this in public? What kind of people are you? This from a people who walk around nude on the beach and whose TV shows more breasts than guns, cars, and beer combined.

Gay, Stephen, and their kids enact a skit showing how Gay and I were arrested at the 1968 Democratic Convention in Chicago. How could they know most of the Bretons supported de Gaulle and opposed the student movement? Still, you'd think the people who produced Talleyrand and gave the world the language and form of modern diplomacy would be better at containing their thoughts, but no. Several are looking at me the way Kathryn did the last time I saw her.

After an hour, the Bretons look battered and bewildered. Marc invites everyone to dinner. It's his birthday, and he's paying for it all—and his guests mock and ridicule him, two of the worst things you can do to anyone in France. How can this be? What kind of people are these? Even his mother joins in. It's too much for them. Madame P orders her son Henri to stand and address the Americans—in English.

"*We* love you, Marc. *We're* glad you're here," and the Bretons, most of whom don't know what he said, applaud—and take over. They sing Breton songs and French songs in solos, duets, combos, and chorus. They quote poems from memory and tell jokes. They dance Breton dances and teach the Americans how to do the steps. At 1:00, Stéphanie carries the cake into the room. People stop dancing and circle it, mumbling. No one has ever seen anything like it. Everyone searches for and finds his or her name, points it out to others, and introduces him or herself. We've been together for five hours, broken bread, shared wine and food, and the ice has finally cracked. The cake is cut, coffee is served, the wine keeps flowing, music blares—The Stones, Beatles, Aznavour, Halliday—and everyone's dancing, men with men, women with women, men with women, kids with anyone, Bretons with Americans.

At 2:30, Madame P goes to the microphone. She and Monsieur, Henri and Renée, and Messieurs Robert, Jacques, and Charles, have bought me a gift. Henri lifts a huge box and places it on the table. I remove the paper without tearing it—to show I'm careful, respectful, frugal, not profligate, and see it's a TV. I'm touched. They've bought a television to keep me company, probably hoping I'll watch it and learn how to speak French, which would make life easier for everyone. Before I have a chance to say anything, Madame P breaks into song and leads a chorus of Bretons singing the Breton national anthem. That's how the evening ends. Good-byes, *à bientôts*, farewells, adieus, everybody laughing. I walk home with my ten housemates, who proceed to finish the roast they started.

The next day I go to the restaurant to pay Stéphanie. She has the bill completely itemized, including every bottle of wine and mineral water and the tip for the two servers. It's a little over six thousand francs, about eleven hundred dollars, twenty-five dollars a person. I don't know how they do it. I thank her and Georges and the staff for a wonderful, memorable night. Then I go home, turn on the TV, and begin to study French. I'm the E. F. Hutton of Brittany. When I speak, people listen. I wish I knew what I said.

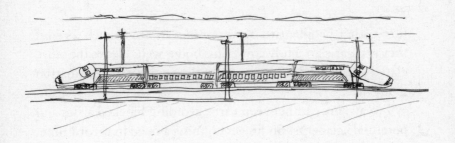

Two Loves, Two Lives

I arrived late last night and unpacked. This morning I have to shop for everything. I begin at Maison de la Presse to buy postcards to send to Donna and select ten sunny photos to remind her what it's like here, sometimes. Three people are wedged ahead of me, and I'm doing my best to wait patiently while the lady in front goes back and forth about something. The man behind the counter, who usually says nothing to me, and didn't say "Bonjour" when I entered, waves me to the front of the line. My first day back, and already I've done something wrong.

I schlep to the counter with my eyes lowered like he caught me stealing and hand him the postcards, saying "Dix." He pushes them away and rings up the sale: fifteen francs. "Merci," I say, and pay him, stunned.

I've been in this store hundreds of times, and this is the first time he hasn't counted the cards. He doesn't even count the money when I hand it to him, and he's served me ahead of three other people, two of whom I know are French, even if they are Parisian. Holy cow! This bodes well. I leave the store elated and go to Leclerc, a continuing source of humiliation in my life.

I weave my cart between carts, avoiding blocked aisles and potential accidents, finding everything I need in record time. My cart is loaded, topped with paper towels, napkins, and toilet paper that I miraculously found in this year's new, hidden enclave. Why they hide these things, I'll never know. Nor, apparently, do the French.

I'm in the soup aisle, which was last year's cereal aisle, checking out the newest soups in a box, when a completely frazzled woman in stiletto heels and dressed as if she's going to the theater, slams her cart into mine and demands—in French—"Where did you get that toilet paper?"

I point to the back of the store and say "En bas," which I know means under, not back, but it's as close as I can get. She thanks me graciously, "Merci, merci, monsieur," and tells me, resignedly, "J'ai cherché pour quinze minutes," then wheels her cart away and bangs into another woman who's searching for something. I'm thrilled. To my great surprise, I knew the answer and helped her, and even more surprising, I knew the question, too!

I'm feeling pretty good as I get in line at the checkout stand—first the Maison de la Presse guy, then the toilet paper lady. I think I'm ready for anything, prepared as a WEBELO, semper fi like the marines. In the past, I've been sent back to reweigh my produce, or worse, had to wait while people in line stared at me as the girl behind the counter left to reweigh my produce, because one look told her and everyone else no matter how many times I weighed it, I'd never get it right. But not today. Today, I've got it. I've correctly weighed my fruit and veggies, pushed all the right buttons on the scale, matched picture, name, and product, distinguished between four types of tomatoes, white and yellow peaches, big and small mushrooms, three kinds of pears, and got all the weights and prices right. Everything is on the checkout stand, arranged from nonedible, heavy, solid, to breakable, bruiseable, fragile, waiting for me to pack. If pride is a sin, I'm already in Hell.

"Bonjour," I say to the girl behind the counter.

"Bonjour," she says, and begins sliding each item across the electronic bar code reader.

I pick up the toilet bowl cleaner and see there are no plastic bags on the counter. "Le sac, s'il vous plaît?" I ask, as I have hundreds of times before.

"Quoi?"

"Le sac?"

She shakes her head, no. A quiver of doubt runs through me. It reminds me of the first summer I was here when I didn't take a cart, didn't think I needed one because I wasn't going to buy much, then did, bought more than I could carry, and grabbed an empty cardboard box and put everything in it. When I got to the counter, the girl stared at me. She points to the box and indicates she's going to charge me for it. "No, no," I say, "Je vole." I'll return it. At least that's what I wanted to say, *volver* being "to return" in Spanish, which even though isn't French is the next country over and European with a Latinate language. "Oui, oui," I affirm, "Je vole." The girl blanches. People in the line step away. It isn't until I go home and look *vole* up in a dictionary that I realize *voler* is to steal, and I was outlandishly, brazenly announcing my theft. The good news is the girl recognized she was dealing with an idiot and didn't charge me for the box or call the gendarme. The bad news is she's there every time I shop, and says "Bonjour" when she sees me and giggles. So I look at *this* girl, determined to be very careful. I know something's up, but I have no idea what, only whatever it is won't be good for me. The bravura I felt a minute ago is gone, along with, apparently, the plastic *sacs*, which until this summer have been as ubiquitous as rain.

"Pollution," she says. "Pas de sac."

"Ah. Bon." I've been worried about France's lack of concern with the environment. There's not much recycling, little wind or solar energy, lots of nuclear power, and everything is packed and packaged in plastic. They're finally doing something about it. Good! I pick up the 25-liter plastic container of laundry detergent called OMO—who knows why?—and place it in my cart.

"Monsieur," the girl says, and points to a dozen large silver-colored plastic bags hanging from a rack behind the register. Oh, no. I should have known. *Free* plastic bags increase pollution; sold plastic bags with the Leclerc *Eco* logo on it are fine. I look at my things on the checkout counter. A quick calculation tells me I'll need at least six bags, and without them packing will take forever. I look at the people behind me, patiently waiting, carrying their shimmering plastic Leclerc Eco bags, and realize I can't do it, that I'll never own such a bag or wear a shirt or glasses or shorts with an alligator on it or buy a pastel-colored T-shirt with a cutesy saying in English or French, like "Be My Friend" or "Je t'aime."

"No, merci," I say to the girl and place the paper towels in the cart after she swipes them across the bar code reader. I do the same with the napkins, toilet paper, and everything else. The woman behind me, a Brit—I can tell by her rumpled blouse and the four liter bottles of gin in her cart—sighs. I do what the French do, take my time and ignore her, though she bothers me, because one look tells me I'm as unkempt as she is, and if I were in her place, I'd act the same, or worse.

I finish packing the cart and pay the bill, counting out a thousand francs in twenty- and fifty-franc notes. I wheel the cart to the car and remove each item and place it securely behind the backseat for the ride home, where I will again remove the items one or two at a time and carry them to the kitchen, bathroom, bedroom, and shed. The good news, I tell myself as I walk back and forth from the car to the house, is I didn't succumb, bow to pressure, and buy the bag like everyone else. The bad news is, I'll never be French.

If this were the end of a story, things would reconcile, add up, *I* would add up, or at least have direction, there'd be no loose ends, and the end might take you back to the beginning. But this isn't a story, it's my life, and the French and American sides don't easily fit. When I'm in France, I see how American I am. In the U.S, it's the reverse. I now try to bring the best of my American self (friendly, active, progressive, persistent, generous, doubting, resilient, prepared, inventive, questioning, analytical, self-mocking, humorous, independent) to France and the best of my French self (trusting, accepting, open, connected, accommodating, patient, respectful, compliant, childlike, living in the present, grateful, dependent, conservative, wondrous) to America, and often fall short in both places.

Here's what I've learned. Two loves and two lives is not an easy life. When something happens here, I worry. When something happens there, I worry. I now worry two times as much as I used to. In that, I find familiarity and purpose. And also in this: *Finistère*, the end of the earth in French, is *Penn ar Bed* in Breton—the beginning of the world. For me, it is.

Acknowledgments

Most books are not written alone, and this book is not an exception. The ways people helped, supported, and assisted are innumerable. I want to thank the following people for making it possible for me to write this book:

❦ ❦ ❦

In France

Yvonne, Yvon, Yann, Xavier, Thierry, Tatjana, Susan, Sharon, Sandy, Raymond, Olivier, Nolwenn, Noé, Monique, Mikael, Martine, Martin, Marion, Marie, Marcel, Maëlle, Ludwig, Louise, Loni, Kerry, John, Joël, Jean-Pierre, Jeanine, Jean, Gilles, Gilbert, Georges, Gaël, Françoise, François, Evelyne, Estelle, David, Claude, Christine, Bruno, Bob, Anjela.

For Reading, Editing, Correcting, and Suggesting— in English, French, Latin, and Breton

Sharon Ahearn, Timmie Chandler, Peggy DeCoursey, Anne Fox, Roy Glassberg, Gilles Goulard, Paula Panich, Janice and Warren Poland, Fred Setterberg, and Kate Vergeer.

For Illustration Ideas

Betty Krasne, Marty Schwartz, and George Wallach

Acknowledgments

For Evocative and Elegant Drawings
Kim Thoman

For Technical Support, Advice, Help, and Hand-holding
Bob Grill

For Numerous Visits to Plombien and Friendship Beyond Reason
Peggy DeCoursey, Joanna Smith, and LeRoy Votto

For Warm, Clean, Cheap, Well-lit Office Space
Bill and Helen Shyvers

For Inspiration, Role Models, and Teachers
Molly Giles, Leo Litwack, and the ongoing creative writing
class at the Downtown Oakland Senior Center

For Publication
Naomi Puro, who found Denis Clifford, who found Phillip
Spitzer, my agent—the best—who found Leslie Meredith,
my editor, also the best. Lucky me.

*For Those People Who Came to the House and the Area and
Who Will Always Be Part of It and Me, Though They Are No
Longer Here*
Patrice Bastard, Jerry and Sheryl Kramer, Pat Schwartz,
Michael Valentini, Eve St. Martin Wallenstein

❧ ❧ ❧

About the Author

MARK GREENSIDE holds B.S. and M.A. degrees from the University of Wisconsin. He has been a civil rights activist, Vietnam War protestor, antidraft counselor, Vista Volunteer, union leader, and college professor. His stories have appeared in *The Sun, The Literary Review, Cimarron Review, The Nebraska Review, Beloit Fiction Journal, The New Laurel Review, Crosscurrents, Five Fingers Review,* and *The Long Story,* as well as other journals and magazines, and he is the author of the short story collection *I Saw a Man Hit His Wife.*

He presently lives in Alameda, California, where he continues to teach and be politically active, and Brittany, France, where he still can't do anything without asking for help.